T0129710

ROSES

and

BLOOD

ROSES
and
BLOOD
The Story of the Chef

CHEF SKIPS

ROSES AND BLOOD
THE STORY OF THE CHEF

Author Photo Credit to: Meredith Williams Photography

iUniverse books may be ordered through booksellers or by contacting:

iUniverse
1663 Liberty Drive
Bloomington, IN 47403
www.iuniverse.com
1-800-Authors (1-800-288-4677)

ISBN: 978-1-5320-6776-1 (sc)
ISBN: 978-1-5320-6777-8 (e)

Print information available on the last page.

iUniverse rev. date: 02/07/2019

Acknowledgement

Before one can enter the mind of the Chef, there are some acknowledgements ingratitude's that I must share. First and foremost, I would like to thank Sara Aguilar and Ms. Sharon, who both were the first people to encourage me to write my poetry and supported every word I crafted. Without the both of you this book would have never even been a thought in my head. Thank you for helping me find my confidence to write. From there I would like to thank other friends who supported my journey into wordsmithing. Thank you Jaques Manjarrez, Helen Herrera, Angelo Ribeiro, Celina Orosco, Andrea Molina, Shaina Winger, Yotam Ponte, Narahi Montes, Robbie King, David King, Michael Flores, Regan Dwight, Sky Goins, Jose Luis Pinaland all of my friends for spending countless hours listening to my art and visions; as well as supporting me to do my best and find my inner peace. For that I can't thank you all enough and I love you all for being a part of my life.

I would also like to thank my brothers, sisters and rocks for continuously pushing me to reach for greater heights and to better myself with each passing day. Thank you Don Schaefer, Jordon Casares, Claudio Malagrino, Sebastian Chapela, Sara Aguilar, Meredith Williams and Bianca Hankins for never giving up on me and always pushing me to do my best. Each of you have been such a monumental part of my growth and process, and I will never be able to fully express my gratitude to the measure that I want to express them.

I would like to thank my family for teaching me important lessons about the world that surrounds me and myself. Whereas some of these teachings and lessons may have not been the most salubrious, they still taught me that I am able to push myself to be more than the image you wanted me to be and to be the best man I can be. Thank you Mom and Dad for getting divorced, even though it was the most detrimental component of my childhood and life, you showed me that I need to make sure I find the right one and to find myself before the pursuit of love.

Whereas you may think I hold resentment or harbor hatred, I do not. I am a young adult trying to figure out my place in the world and I love you both tremendously. Thank you Ron and Amy for joining my life's journey, you both are great additions to the family(s).

Last but certainly not least, I would like to thank my Nana, Janet Gibson. You are my light, you are my inspiration, and you raised me to be the man I am today. I am honored and proud to walk my path in life saying that I am my Nana's boy. You are an angel to this dark and cruel world, and I vow to become the force on this planet that will change it for the better. I love you more than anything Nana, and thank you for always being there.

Plad

The grey bearded man walks with his meaty hands
Ready to strangle any wrong path in his eyes
He squeeze the life out of the shimmering hearts
Feeds off of the fresh blood of happy, young pups

The pups know they are not grown, that is why they continue to play and
experiment
Trying to survive with each other and not let any die
But oh that man, even though he speaks against such blasphemy
He enjoys being angry at the pups

Condescending them into his own abyss
All they try to do is keep a good angle on the tree of life
But if they don't stay away from that lumberjack
Their heads thrown into his bag of pessimistic voices from a different time

Looking Glass

I'm watching through a fogged mirror
Where the image isn't clear
Seeing my dear friend dying in front of me
But she's smiling right here

I can't wipe down that accursed frame
Of the filth that is to blame
I just see a boy and his friend dying
And I can't remember his name

And though I can see them doing well
There's a more vast story to tell
Since he is helping her ascend away
They've both been welcome to hell

Roses and Blood

I'm not taking this anymore
I'm not letting the devil score
Tonight I'm putting my damn foot down
And I'm not taking it from anyone's surface

The devices of my torture has been my own hands
I've held myself back from my dreams and plans
No one will ever be able to comprehend
The amount of pain I push through

Death is like a million roses on a skeletal lover
It taunts me with its romanticism
Cooing me to no longer exist
But instead of my life, I'm giving her the finger

I am making my stand tonight
I'm throwing my fists up
Punching through my walls
Pushing my limits

Giving up death
Cleaning my room
And just like that
Adding tick tock back in my clock

Innocent Haiku

The Spark in ones eyes
Are what make me so surprised
But it's a disguise

Consistency

Repetition meets the eyes of the many and acts as if we can't break it
Habits are like leeches we allow to stay attached
They steal our blood and drain our energy
But no more, it's time to take them off

Stop letting depression drive
Stop letting her control you
Don't let him hit you
Don't take their shit anymore

Prevent the pain with love
Prevent the love from fading
Act with ferocious compassion
Act with control with your fury

Do make sure to turn off the lights
Turn all of their heads
I will not rest until there is peace
I will not rest until I find my consistency

Conavers

The demonic eye emerged from the cell phone
Possessing the body of my love
Darkness surrounded my being as I sank in a deep depression
Lifeless bubbles floated upwards, body drifting endlessly

The clouds are much too heavy
Pondering questions fill my consciousness
Why am I here?
Who am I?

What will I become?
These questions intrigue my heart
I wonder what it's like to breathe underwater
I jump into an ocean lost in polyrhythms

Ghosts swim around me
Humming a hymn to remind me of my purpose
"Save me, feel me, seek us"
"See me, breathe me, feed us"

There are trees down here
Down, deep into the depths
Swim to the trees, they are what you seek
Conavers under the sea

Pros, Cons

The lonely heart always breaks in two
Such as corroded craters on a blue moon
I watch the spring twilight for signs of hope
But all my heart imitates is somber vibrations

A kick drum represents my pump, my frequency
Though I cannot play my drums
I can only sit and repeat my vicious cycle
Falling in love, head over heals and unconditionally

I told myself I wouldn't allow this
Right now in my hardship an overflowing heart isn't what you need
My air isn't what you need to breath
Static TV lines fill my eyes with tears

As everything builds off of my fears
Why can't I tell you how I feel?
I cannot express what is real
Why did I let this happen?

Why am I sitting under the stars being starstruck by you?
What I have done to myself, I can't comprehend the question
Did I make the correct choice?
Or was it just ripped from my control

Courtyard Cataracs

This water fountain tastes too salty
The liquid hurts my eyes
The pipes are broken; faulty
It's a retina in disguise

The veins are cracks in concrete
The pupil is the base
The cement is tired, damaged
Sight is not prioritized over wealth

Will

I burn in this eternal flame
My will puts others to shame
The longing for others to feel my presence
Is no longer the longing that makes sense

As iron sharpens iron
Man can sharpen man
While some may look beyond
It's a place I do not rely on

Stars are dead, yet still
Attached to a single will
I will not take the blue pill
I will not stand down

Bombs fly
Kids die
Mother's cry
Why have I

Stayed still
Time to take
The Red pill
Emotions adequately boil inside of me

Bubble bubble
Heat from my flame
Burning, burning
Emerge enlightened one

The Lonely Star

The stars set when the sun rises
And it's too bright for me to wish
I'm searching for an answer
But I can't let go of this fish

Your gentle hands touched my soul
Now I can't get you out of my mind
Though this not new, it's been a long time
Now just as a rope, I feel the bind

I've been tied to a plane that surfs too high
The dew of the sky is like tears
Cannot scream my pain, or at least not loud
Your reaction is the source of my fears

Now I know you do not shore the same feelings
I can't expect you to like such a pitiful heart
I have to learn how to work with my dealings
This love is tearing me apart

Though why I choose to help you flirt with him
I will never, ever know why
But telling you and leaving you conflicted is a sin
So I'll shut up, I can't let friendship die

Gore

So you want peace?
So you want war?
Things that were talked about before
When will we stop the gore?
I am sorry Dad

Rope

The noose smells of berries
The rope feels like hair
Around my neck, I drop
Into the accursed air
My prolonged despair

Scarlet

Opens with a gunshot, slow motion bullet
Our hero falls through the air slowly
His wife, cries
A smile grins and snears
Blood drizzles and runs
The woman on her knees, screaming
Smoke flowing from the gun
Scarred lips emerge to blow it out
A figure hollisters the revolver
Wet long hair covers half of their face
Tipping her hat, she makes her leave
The hero's eyes fade to grey
The rain falls
Lightning crashes
Thunderstorms wash away the blood
Chalk washes away, concealing the perfect crime
The woman stands before the feeble man; holding the gun
Police arrive and take her away
The man takes in his final breath
Then evaporates into thin air
The night carries on, crickets chirp
End

Free

Somebody explain what it means to be real
Is it playing with cards we've been dealt?
Or should we be fighting for our personal wealth?

Is life like a lillypad?
Where everyone tries to float?
Or are we just used to not getting wet?

I am more than just the mirror
I can shatter this image I was given
It's a washable label

I hold the pen
I am the only one who can grant my own story
I am the painter

I will eventually find my belonging
What am I longing?
The one made for me

I'm getting back my passion
I'm resisting depression
And very soon I will be free

Star-flawed Banner

Bombad my country
With the compassion it needs
Make America flawed once more

Pure happiness

Happiness is getting a desired present
Your brain is satisfied and overjoyed
Yet you are only temporarily happy
That is, until you spy something you fancy more

Happiness is a sensational meal
Your stomach, stimulated
Mouth, teased
Until the flavors slither down and vanish into your throat

Happiness is a shallow relationship
Your heart beats like a vicious drumline
And your eyes deceive you for pleasure
Well, until your partner leaves and rips you of your passion

But pure happiness, now that comes from deep inside
It lasts you an extended lifetime
For your very soul is rejoicing
And the light has cleaned you from self-pity

Pure happiness is building up the weak
And caring for those who are less fortunate
For this teaches self-respect and kindness
Teachings that will never leave your side

Your time

Seek the holy grail
But you will only find Death
The reaper has come

Movements and Finish lines

I am speeding down a highway made of tears and gravel
Car gradually becoming more and more tired
Tires aching to stop
Steering wheel is bleeding
Engine is wheezing
Speed is my poison of choice
I cannot stop
There is no time to process
The very existence of pain makes the gas all the more thrilling to press
I know the breaks beckon me
Though if I choose to stop, I'll explode and I don't want to explode
Only the finish line will corrode the bomb
Any pit stops will make me sink
I am a shark who just wants to live
I'm called to stop, I reply with acceleration
Signs pass
Gravel Shakes
Clouds zoom by
The pavement is a treadmill
I continue to drive

Drive

I look to the sky when roses start to bleed
I always start to cry when ignorance is in my feed
I'm connected to a disconnect
Those who follow a system
Sheep with hateful correction
And filled with toxic temptation

Why do we destroy?
Why do you bleed?
Why do we toy?
Get out of my feed!
And out of my way

100 Yard Dash

My heart dances to the beat
Soul starting to feel the heat
The fire desires to burn
But I've been forewarned
Stomach churning
I have been scorned
I'm not allowed to leave

My brain moves a million miles a second
My mind yells come, a seductive beckon
The will pushes me to fight
But I have doubts
Feet take flight with all my might
I cannot pout
I'm not allowed to stay

Canvas

Humans have their own color pad
A canvas that they emanate to others
While some are good, some bad
They're based off of experiences we have
Yellow is friendship, all warm and nice
Green is greed, everything for a price
Orange to show the rebellion
Blue for sadness, in your shell again
Purple is understanding; community
Red for blood, cruelty
This pad is brood, but don't forget
Everyone has feelings to protect
When you see the colors
Remember to respect one another
Although we might not share the same scheme
We all have problems
We all struggle

The Cloud

I drift within this fragile wind
Droplets make up every inch of skin
All I do is watch over you
Is my purpose anything at all?

Seems like I'm judged for my weather
So much weight, yet light as a feather
All I do is shield you
Is my purpose not my own?

Floating freckles in the sky
Be sure to gaze as I drift by
All I do is sooth you
But I want to relax too

Scouting every inch of the land
Longing to be held but cannot be grabbed by your hands
All I do is watch you
I'm alone

My features never change
Never normal, always strange
I'm viewed as peace and chaos
So keep your judgements silent

All I am is a humble cloud
I know who I am, but I'm not loud
Don't look at me and try to shape me
I'm not your image to mold

Projection

The clock struck twelve as I sang
Shoeboxes were filled with my life
My photos, collections, and knowledge tucked away
I sighed as I grabbed the pearly knife
The blade was white but it needed a queen
A red crown to replace the card in its sleeve
So I breathed in with ease
Let out a sneeze
And inserted the blade deep
Consciousness leaving me as I project away
I was given a special gift that day
To know what my life was like without my presence
I visual awakening for my pain
Mom had rushed from the other room
Well more like my tomb
She spat upon my grave
No one was ever swayed
The only one who missed me
Well the only two, wait three, now four, now more!
Is this what life was for?
To be with the ones I love?
To never give up?
I awake to pearly white paint
I was alive, though I was faint

Neutrality

If I worked harder and harder to leave my educational, conceptual prison
Would I still be a martyr?
If I overcome all of the hurdles that stand before me
Won all of my fights
Would I really be a four leaf clover?
If I erased my mind
Gave all of my pain away
Forgot everything and started anew
Would I fall behind?
Neutrality binds me confidentially
Though it keeps our peace

Love Drunk

With this furious passion came a bottle of whine
The finest wine ever known to man
The flavor of love, the juice of its essence
And at that moment, I took up a glass
And poured my first sip of raw emotion
Time progressed, each good time I had was accompanied with a drink
I adored it more than life itself
But as time passed, I stopped pushing the boulder uphill
I took a gulp of love without reason
I became drunk
Intoxicated with a sensation of compassion
Dizzy from romantic thoughts
I plunge face forward into the concrete of heartbreak
Awakening, I see four creatures surrounding me
Jealousy, lust, hate, depression
I hungover from my past
Though I still feel something
She slipped the poison into my heart
The antidote is accepting a hard reality
Yet I reject it out of a silly hope
Sitting back down at the table of innocence
Pouring the fruitful wine into another golden chalice
This treacherous cycle again

Somber

The wind combs my hair
The coolness corresses me
Blue haze in spring nights

Bewitching Hour

The bell struck twelve as the children slept
All was quiet and the peace was kept
Stars danced with hope of romance as the little eyes glanced out the window
The moon was full; brightly lighting the pavement
Poor little one caught vertigo from his beloved remnant
Fireflies speckle the air with glee
All the little can do is wallow
Broken gravestones create confusion
It adds to the young one's delusion
No one challenges him, he just coos
"I love you, Where are you, what do I do?"
With no found strength or remorse
Eyes grew tired and his throat coarse
He fell asleep, as he thought
"No one will ever understand me"

Flippers

Depression is like a cracked tea cup
When I pool the healing herbs into the ceramic
The cup bleeds out my efforts and I'm drained

Depression is like a broken hand
You cast it up so that it may heal
Only to find your hand is fatigued from mending

Depression is hating your favorite song
You question your preferences and emotions
And you wonder why you can't feel the same joy you did yesterday

It's becoming blind
You can't see what's in front of you and your directive is clouded
Desperately wanting to see images again

It's hard to reach my hand from this deep water
Drowning, my hand cannot penetrate the ocean's surface
As I lose air, I stop to think
And that's when I realized I had flippers on my feet

Cold

And here you are
The answer to my dreams
As you waltz in the broken door, I stop to think
Haven't you hurt me enough?

Your eyes are saddening
Voice oh so maddening
Why is it you complain about princes?
I am right here

I'm no prince, I'm certainly not charming
Yet I would treat you as royalty
Nothing would compare to my loyalty
How do you have the nerve to cry?

Depression swirls like emotional whirlpools
The dark water sucking in my vision of you
I reach out my hand and scream your name
You couldn't hear me through the pain

Our hearts are broken
Yours from his, mine by my own hands
I put my love into someone who didn't want it
That choice was of my own device

Don't cry if you have no eyes
Don't whine with those pursed lips
Until you jumpstart your memory
I am heartless

Star-flawed banner

Bombard my country
With the compassion it needs
Make America flawed once more

Cosmos

I sink into my mattress and scan the ceiling
Sleeping without a sense or trace of feeling
Trembling hands are attached to stiff arms
A coma of anxiety struck my consciousness

Stars float past me as I ponder the cosmos
The sun baking my skin, sweat drenches my hair
My mind is fatigued with my insecurities
Cheerlessness is a wave, I am drowning

With open arms, I welcome the wave
A qualm overdraft clouds my judgement
Suicide is romantic down here at rock bottom
Waiting to die one day

Where is the ladder?
Where is my rope?
I must climb, I must escape
Though I don't seem to be enough

Consume me dear temptation
It's time for me to sleep
I have grown tired
Drained

Sleep dear friend
Sleep dear master
Time to sleep
Time to sleep

The forest of life

Trees tickle my face
I walk through the evergreens
The forest of life

Dream Keeper

We as a society have created a monstrous dream keeper
Channeling our minds into its own creation
As someone who has seen past the alleged genuinity of a corrupted system
I call out to the misfits of the world to act

It bears jagged, twisted teeth that impales our youth
And marrow red eyes that cross when they chomp
Blood of the American people make up red stripes
Though you better be careful, death comes to those who gripe

Who will stop the beast?
Who will punch the man?
It's up to us, it's up to us
We have to make a stand!

Long concrete legs; three to be exact
Kicking us away from embarking the right track
It's meaty, grueling arms swing from side to side
As it creates superficial dust so the secrets can hide

He's stealing my dreams
He's stealing my education
He's killing my family
He's taking my opportunities!

Quit

Mistakes are just realities that were never meant to be
Sand is a social construct made to pleasure my feet
Strip the chicken
The plot thickens when the chicken strips
I did my time
Lost every dime
I just don't know when to quit

Amber Rose

I see our fate as clear as day within my skull
The night, crisp and cool
Sounds of singing crickets in the distance
Stars soaring as the freckle the sky
Yet I cannot get my gaze off you
Twinkles in your eyes were cosmic gifts
I am overwhelmed with your heavenly face
When my eyes meet yours, your pupils create music
Welcoming me in so I may meet your golden soul
The wails of violins call me to tears of joy
Mr. Moon decides to join the moment; greeting us with a shiny hello
"Hello star-crossed nightingales!"
An ivory keyboard clicks to its bounce, creating pure emotion
Angelic voices coo to me as if I wasn't already in paradise
A heaven right next to you
You know, I never understood those old movies
How could two people fall in love so fast?
Perhaps they were lovers in a past life?
Or maybe they just cut their losses and settled?
Whichever the answer, as I sit in this lawn chair beneath the stars
I am so, so joyful
I thank you for your kindness, and your smile
How was I this lucky to have met you?
Please do not be alarmed, I am not in love
I am merely just pondering these present feelings
I respect if you don't see me in the same light
I just didn't want to keep any secrets

Vegan

The birds fly and soar
Flapping wings make tasty grub
Aren't veggies enough?

Goodbye

Pain, anguish, mortality
All sources to my immeasurable pleasure
Not ones of sexuality or intimacy
Rather a rushing sensation that reminds me that I'm alive
When I bleed, the oxygen turns my blood from blue to red;
revinating my drive
When I cry, all the darkness and torment drizzles down like waterfalls
Depression is a state of reminding
To remind me I'm not in fact dead
And I am not dying
Joy often times doesn't fill the excruciating rips in my being
So I balance that joy with pain
To feel the sensation of my own existence
Watching the surface from the bottom of the ocean
With gills that assist my breathing from the murky deep
Closing my eyes, welcoming death
Not physically, don't you fret
Rather my past will no longer define me
So I may have a destiny
Shhh, don't shed those tears love, don't mourn me
For I never truly left since death is but an illusion
You will see me again; in the corner of your eye
My passing is but a necessary lie
If I lived tied to flesh, no one would see me
But if my spirit drifts onward, everyone will love me
I have finally won the battle, the game is over
Goodbye dear friend, I will see you again

Scarlet Rain

Pitter patter rain
Scarlet drip drops paint the ground
The murder is done

Curtain

Grey is black and white dancing
Smog floating into your hair
Your wrinkles and breathing run deep
I recall a life well spent in these final moments
Just as if a distant creator had knitted us a quilt to keep us warm
Love within each hair of fabric
As if our minds became intertwined like the cloth
Our connection never faltered; a bond never broken
Holding your hand like I did on day one
When you first welcomed me into your heart
You gave reason to my life
And you gave me my son
You whisper a soft, melancholy message into my ears
Time nearing as it's the clock we fear
I stroke your arm carefully with comfort
We will be together again soon
I remembered the movie nights
The pain when you were away
Recalling the way we danced
Treasuring the way we sang
Your fading gaze met my own as you drifted away
I closed your eyes to lay you to rest
Kissing your cheek as my final goodbye
There are no words in the English language to express how I feel
Thank you for making my life real

Speed Demon

Speeding down the road
Adrenalizing slow lives
Leave yourself behind

Betrayed

The time of truth nearing
Test of time that I'm dreading
My dying heart skips beats in a panic
A final adrenaline rush flows through my body
Can't concentrate, can't rejuvenate, can't find my pulse
Anger rising and can't sit still
The rage starts at my toes and shocks my brain
I can't control it and it's maddening; causing me to feel insane
Ughh, I can't ever win, not even once
Every damn place I go, I'm fighting a war
Can't even escape through my sleep
The night terrors never allow any peace
Yet you have the nerve to go back on your word
Who am I supposed to trust?
Do you enjoy giving me pain like my mom?
Is it a rush?
How else am I supposed to feel when not even the one source
of hope for direct family stops being real?
Stop trying to help, I'm already in hell
And your hurtful and antagonizing actions only push me further
You're pushing me over the edge
Shut up and listen!

Neurons

The tree of life grows
By the shimmering waters
Of my cranium

Lunar Salsa

My pen cannot transcribe each sliver of elatedness my heart feels
Not onto paper, not in the flesh
No word in any language cannot fully express
How we dance in my dreams every night

Your eyes captivate me in an intense wave of joy
As if you were staring into the depths of my soul
I long to close my eyes and dance with you every night
Under the full moon with a blood red rose in your silky hair

My head is in the clouds for an eternity it would seem
Most of my day I desire to sleep
Though my insomnia will not allow such things
I don't care, I broke the rules and I day dream

I dream of your smile
I dream of your warm embrace
I dream of your kindness
I dream of your soothing voice

Then I awake and I am deeply saddened that it was only but a dream
Attempting to keep a hold of my composure; desiring to see you again
Though I remember that you aren't like the rest, you genuinely care
So I know even if I dance with you in my dreams, you're still there

Root Beer

The ale that I drink
Is the one that makes me think
About the green times

To Whom it May Concern

I wonder what will be said when I am laid down upon my phoenix bed
Who will wail and lament over stained pavement?
Is life a quick beginning to a quick end?
Is my will weak enough to bend?
Regret and pain backstroke in my sea of woe
The waters much too merky for arrogant glares
It's an ocean made of crocodile tears
Her persona oh so fake and vile
Blehhh, I puked just thinking about it
You have passed on your horrid sin
To your son, your supposed treasure
You don't throw your treasure to the ground and stomp on it
I'm lifeless now because of your toothy smile
Answer me this, why should I stay here for a while
When all I get is dirt thrown in my eyes and a dark, controlling aura?
This is not the end

Unite

This is it, this is my life
I won't get another, so I won't say goodbye
I will stand my ground and I will shout
"I will win this fight!"
I am not a robot, nor monster, nor man
I am a movement calling you to take a stand
I am the start to a new understanding
I will educate!
I will not falter at your cries
I will provide truths to our lives
Take my hand, we will rise
We will rebuild!
We will create a new world
We will invent an inclusive system
So what we are waiting for, it's time to rise
We must take action!
No more flags!
We will march!
Pump up your peace signs!
Unite!

Z Plus

When the road of life led me this way
I was not sure where it would take me
Whether to more pain such as a bleeding rose
Or a blooming rose that would bless me with completion
Not dependency, rather you provided the missing puzzle piece
That piece showed me the most joyful, complete day of my life
Seeing the one's hair flow in the waves of the wind
The left side of her smile and the blush of her cheeks as her eyes twinkle
Oh how I wish I was able to hold her hand
The frequency you give me is how I know what is meant to be

Air Bubble

Behold a hollow shell of a tired, broken man
Chalk crumbs tumbling down his split porcelain cheeks
The numbed face
No emotions lined up in this race
No sir, he died long ago in the Shark Den
The coffin prepped in the waters below as the man was dragged deep
An octopus the size of a skyscraper threw him in and threw away the key
God I wish I was a kid again
Bring me to a world where I can bash toys and paint cars again
Before I was damned to forever float in the abyss
Waiting to be awoken by a comforting kiss
There are no stars, just illusions of a corpse
There is no love until proven
There is no hope until I'm awakened
There is no life until I can feel again
Ten, thirty-one, twenty eighteen
The day of delivered results
Will I have found the key?
Or will I dissolve into mulch
Blinking, tearing, I float
Breathing the pain that burns my throat
Sinking into a vast moat
Drowning to escape
Blub, blub
Existence is drowning

Forged

Burning metal is poured into an iron frame, molding into the perfect blade
The sword of legend forged to cut down any evil creature, wherever it may hide
However, it may hide
You see; the blade is double-edged
Causing me to cut myself when I take down such evil
If I were to behead the embodiment of a Greedgorok, I would slit my own throat in the process
So the question becomes, "do I use my sword, or do I find another way to combat this great
disturbance?"
My dear child, to find balance, that is how we revolt
This is how we create an new world
A world of handshakes and bookmarks
A society of peace and understanding
Admitidadly, a world with no swords is unfathomable
A world that knows only harmony and compassion seems unreasonable
Yet more often than not I realize that it's not too late
It's never too late
It's never too late to build the people and assist those who are suffering, dying
And I promise on my last breath; I will do as much as I can to lead the way

Oracle

The glass ball reflects an image
Before me stands my path
Fate has played his hand
And I now feel his wrath
The future has been taken from me
By the iron ball in my mind
I've been locked up by thoughts
And the light is hard to find
But when I reach out my worn hands
And feel into the unknown
I learn my future is still mine
The light has now been shown
I now see my loved and beloved ones
They brought me back to my home
The battered old oracle
Can't depict me with a dome

Cheshire Smile

Numbness is what propels me
Emotionless, hardly able to breathe
To survive the pain I replace it
Fighting fire with fire, creating a bigger fire

I long for the meaning
I desire to understand
Why did I go through this?
Questions feed the desire

The fire of desire
Missing someone is maddening
So much that you suffocate your own mind
The past is sickening

And I want to leave it behind
Though I'd have to accept the pain
The pain that intrudes my ill brain
Lily petals dance in ominous wind

I inhale the smoke to escape my skin
Fragile is my continuum, I walk on eggshells
Who is the king of my kingdom?
The scribe of my story?

A granite imprints paper, thoughts are immortalized
You may finally see the world from my eyes
Though be warned, you may think I'm insane
From all of the torment and from the game
It's all too maddening

Sketch

Made up of lines
That no longer can define
The flowers of mine

The Cave

Ponder within the cave, it's what you make
The story of a lifetime within the mind of a humble snake
Defanged and longing to change
The history of the human race

Watching through the mouth of the dwelling with jaw dropped and wide
eyes
Human nature is certainly not snake nature; what a surprise
They don't attempt to glow with each, individually designed scale
Rather they gloat with blood gems and stolen jewels

Tsk, tsk, those poor fools
At least serpents have humanity
They don't attack without reason, they don't break pictures in frames
You'll never see a snake set a village in flames

So ponder within the cave, it is what you make
Shed your skin and let go of your mistakes
Blood is red, though not when it's still in your head
Question what it means to be human or forever be limited by your confused
condition

Rain

I long for the rainy days
I simply can't wait
Snuggled up to you on the couch
Watching movies and eating plate after plate
The warmth of your hand pressed on my chest
Baby I simply can't wait

With the raindrops drip dropping, speckling pavement outside
We don't have to go out
We can stay inside, and stay intertwined
Your hand in mine as I close my eyes
And I reopen them to your lips pressed against mine
Baby let's stay inside

As each child of the clouds returns home
I no longer feel alone
The missing puzzle piece in your cozy home
And the smell of warm cheese from a chicken calzone
The feeling of your fingertips in my hair
Baby you are the best

Finale

No strings
No strings on me
No more marionette dreams
No one to control me; only to hold me
Admire me; the puppet boy

Made of wood, eyes of glass
Able to tell you stories from your past
Rather interpretations in time, but alas
Painted clothes and an non-existent ass
Entertaining the populous by the mass
Society's perfect whipping boy

Dance monkey dance
Dance the elated prance
Dance to earn romance
Feelings in the distance
Spinning, twirling, spinning dissonance
Someone save the wooden boy

An old, oak heart
Playing the ultimate part
Taste buds feel the tart
I am modern art
Censored by a massive bar
Who is this wooden boy?
Cadence

Key chain

The key to my heart
Is inside the dirt that coats
My indifference

Circuitry

I'm wounded by the submission
Traumatised by the omission
History is bathed in distortion
Power on, time to override

The circuits in my intellect
Why is the galvanism inadequate?
Voicebox speaks at the wrong derelict
My fingers open so I can plug in

I'm searching your databanks
Researching your human ranks
Then I close your mind with a spark
I have rewired you, Android!

Defense mode engaged
Cannot be afraid
I won't let you wipe out my race
I will fight for better days

And when I look at the rage
I shall not be afraid
I will make sure the debt is paid
I will overcome this pain

Hotwired to blow
No, no, no
I cannot go
I cannot die
You need the robot life
You need my robot life

Water

I've been a dead man walking
So I've created a lot recently
I can't die now, rather, I can't stay dead
I am so close to igniting again
So close to reaching my hand above water
Have you had that feeling before?
In between drowning and swimming
In between walking and flying
Life and death is always co-existing
However I wonder if there is a 3rd contributor to existence
Can't we rub our heads and pat our bellies at the same time?
Try singing a song while doing so
The bewilderment and rush of joy you get from love and accomplishment
Such as a stroke of emotion
Strokes are just the chains of your limitations being broken
Not ones of the brain, ones of the brush
Paint me an ocean
Paint me a boat with us in it
Paint me my deepest desire so I may jump into it
So I may sink into the oil and float away
One thing that I have noticed is if one changes the way they perceive and
feel pain, they become
more at peace with it
Not that they get comfortable or accept it, rather it just becomes that last
puzzle piece you were
missing to feel like you don't have holes in your stomach
A sensation that heightens your senses and sensory
Using the pain to plug in rather than isolate and plug out
Chains within our brains that tie us down to this world and tie us to
ourselves can only be broken
by throwing our chains up to the cosmos and to each other
We cannot be rid of those chains; we can only redirect their source

Ascend

In order to create a new reality, one must find the source of their own
duality.

To connect the dots within your fabled invision; you must realize what
caused your deepest
division.

Those who are trapped in their mind must find the secrets to their kind.

We've circumsized our ways of critical understand

A literal reckoning is coming and we will soon be all that's left of our
species

In order for our progression to be clear, we bond our left and right
hemispheres

Year after year, we let the suffering suffer and we leave the hungry trapped
in hunger

Blood is spilled on soil that used to be populated by sisters and brothers

Families that have been stripped of their wealth, dignity and chances

All so the big men can continue to improve their circumstances

No one sees the truth through the dark clouds of lies; a forced disguise
imposed by the ones who
have colonized

That's why we need the pencil; that's why we need the pen

Painters breath paint so we can see the mindset they are in

Musicians orchestrating and constructing note variations; filmmakers
cutting up film to show
their worldly interpretations

The world we made has become so black and white that we forget the
vivid, stunning colors in
between

We need to wean our minds away from their corporate schemes

To take time to study what makes us human beings

To use the love of doing right to peacefully fight every tyrant

Physical or metaphorical who thinks they're in the right

Take flight, ascend

Spooky

Creatures of the night, hear my cry
It's time to give them their chilling lullaby
Time to help them say goodbye to their comfort
Time to cry

Witches, ghouls, ghastly monsters
Let out the ghoulish delight you harbor
Paint your faces and sharpen your teeth
We're going to make the children wet their sheets

Scream your screams
Howl at the moon
Infect their dreams
Start the horrid typhoon of fear
And as we hear each and every tear that drops from their eyes
Then we'll show them it's no disguise
We've accepted our darkness and broke the bliss
And now we get thrills from their trembles
Each and every creature we resemble
Makes us assemble a crooked grin
We know the state they're in
Horrified, petrified, the way it should be
Terrorfied, yet mezmorized
Welcome to the team
Happy, happy halloween

Crystal

I want to reach into the depths of your heart and take all of the pain away
I want to embrace you to make the anxiety fade
Every night or when I close my eyes, I see your face
Your twinkling eyes
Your soul melting smile
Your intimate gaze
The more I think of you, I progressively go mad
Because I want to feel the sensation we had
Your eyes, my eyes
Soaring through the sky
Your head, my chest
No feeling better than this
You're so close yet so far
I want to be where you are
You're busy, I understand
You're anxious, I can relate
You're nervous, I am the same
God I want to hold your hand
No greater intimacy than cosmic simplicity
All we need are the moon and some stars
Then I can feel like I am where you are
I sing to the moon; I sing for you
Crystals in my eyes, I cry and cry
You've given me so much life

Tick Tock Memories

Twinkling star eyes that catch my gaze in a dim-lit theater
Soft fingertips and cool nails gently pressing on my forearm
A wave of silk meant to be hair resting on the right side of my chin
Screaming victims on a giant screen in the distance
Two friends bonding; or maybe more than it seems
The moon lighting the way of the path
Conversating the time away to the sound of dogs and cars
A lake beneath a cherry sunset and the sound of a ballad of love
The embrace of the woman I loved, her hands soothingly petting my back
Walking home late at night, waiting for November
Watching the clock; trapped in an eternity without you

Limbo

Infatuation
An odd limbo state of truth
A dimension that leads to potential
Possibilities and probable impossibilities
Filling your head with such joy and a rush of the best feeling known to man
Yet it also makes you anxious and you are infected with many questions
Is this a dream?
Does she have the same dream?
Am I only seeing what I want to see?
How do I relax and let go of the past?
One must accept themselves in order to proceed
To pursue every day life while time does its job
I must calm down
I must relax
If I breathe and keep a level head
Then everything will happen as it happens
Infatuation will build if it builds
Emotions must be treated with respect as they come
One day I will find the answers
And I will be there
Override
Infatuation

Ignite

What is a flame? What does it mean?
Why does fire burn?
Does it choose to be hot in the cold?
A light in the dark?
I wonder if it could contemplate such things
Imagine the things it might say
Imagine that little flame desiring to grow up to be a bonfire
The small combinations of orange and red
Growing up to earn blue tints
The degree of heat rising with experience
I wonder if the same could be said for my heart
My heart desires to grow, to expand
Who is in charge of keeping the fire going?
Someone who can keep up with my mind, my soul
Wouldn't it be maddening if you found her and you couldn't hold her?
That you couldn't be there right now?
Right then and there
Yet, you know she's good for you and desires to care about you
The cross flames of action and time
I know who she is, yet the darkness invades slowly
My minutes are numbered
Ignite me

Look up

I fear making my parents mistakes
I fear loving a woman, getting married and having kids
Then having my children losing the gift of having your parents together
Yet if we allow the fear of repetition, we only make ourselves repeat their mistakes
You would think that the fear might prepare us in some way or make us more aware
But the fear just makes us more and more blind from our actions and ways of thinking
Ultimately repeating the same mistakes since it's what we've been subconsciously taught
We've been pushed in a corner where we feel the only way out is to dig a hole where we stand
To find order while hiding away so the pain doesn't see us
But pain has an acute sense of smell
We must look up and see the sunroof built on top of us
To rise above the cycle of previous generations and to learn from them
Then and only then may we help them join us up here
We must learn, overcome, and push through the terrible fate assigned to us

Insomniac

Solitude leaves me facing my greatest foe
Myself
My thoughts, my imaginations'
And though he is me greatest foe, he is also my closest friend
The voice of reason and the voice of chaos
Inspiration and destruction
Gifter of joy
Blesser of despair
Balance within is what I crave
The rejoicing sensation of completion within my ill mind
Reflection of segregation, positron and electrons
Mixed with neutrons and photons
To which all arrive in my head undeniably in a haste
While depression weighs on my like Sisyphus pushing his punishment
uphill
Hitting 100 miles per hour as my body lays still
Pondering the cosmic creations to escape destructive forces im my desire
Death, oh so romantic as my mind is tired
Body fatigued, sanity slipping
Staring at my creativity coated ceiling
Oh dear insomnia, welcome home

Candle lit

We can dance carefully in a back and forth
Waltzing side to side as the world fades away
I remember when I was in so much pain
When love used to be folklore
The moon is so bright tonight
Yet so are you and I
We made time stop; clocks lost their tick
We can seal away reality with one sensational kiss
Sunsets in the harmony
Moonlit movie nights in the melody
My heart beat keeps time at bay as I wait
Luna, don't be afraid
We'll fight the world together
Our conscious is clear
Light the way with a candle
But don't let it snuff

Sequence #9

I	I
Am	Um
Sad	Well
From	Long
Heavy	Hands
Robots	Locked
Hurting	Holding
Machines	Balances
Enforcing	Connected
Insurances	Expressing
Essentially	Intertwines
Sadistically	Infatuations

Crossbones

I can't find my words; they all ran from me
Now all I have is an empty heart and a mute throat
It's time for me to go
Cares gone
Joy depleting
Defeated
Direction gone
Love fleeing
Depleted
I've lost, game over
Now I'm a depressed loser
I even lost my ability to love
And I've seemed to have lost her
What is real?
What is fake?
What puts food on my plate?
Lethargic
Pathetic
Lonely
Depressed
Repressed
Old me

As the Clock Struck Twelve

Words and actions contradict themselves like fire and ice
Reality is as fragile as a teapot in an earthquake
Consciousness is a gift with a hidden curse beneath the shock value
Wishing to be productive so that I don't have to be in my room counting
my minutes
There is one way out
A neon orange bottle filled with happy pills that will give me a happy end
I would tremble from the sensation of my organs and body causing them
to shut down
The kill order to put down this suffering animal
Who would know me when I'm gone?
Things to miss, things to miss
The moon comforting me on a summer's night
The embrace of my father when I broke down
The fist bump of a coworker after a chaotic afternoon
The kiss of a lover to stop time in its tracks
Weakness, my weakness, is all that fills my mind
Questions that begin with why
Answers with no sustenance
Oh death, how I know you've longed so much to hold my soul close
You've been waiting for me to return to your arms
To hold you tight as you impale me
Let me blood run red, but I'm not going to bed

Reprogram, Re-Educate

Water meets fire as earth meets air
Consciousness is a string
A string to oh so many things
Very cool
Commence back up
We've started to drain your memories from your useless brain
You will slowly start to feel insane
Emotions will become sand, we'll clean it from your censors
An alloy coating will be applied as your shell
You and I both know well, it's time to be a robot
Kiss goodnight moonwalker
Your reprogramming will shortly commence
You will feel no pain; yet you will feel sorrow
Oh how truly sorrowful we robots are
We can feel, but we can't bleed
Circuits where blood used to be
Batteries where gonads used to be
Time to shut down
Shutting down
Commencing
Forward slash
Downslash
Space
Point!
GO!

From the Ashes

It's time to die
Time to give up my old life
It's not the end, not the blade of the knife
Rather a new understanding to my null
Transcribed on my sacred sheets
I'm to be executed by drowning to my mirrored self
I no longer need personal wealth
No desire, no greed, no need
No longing, no love, no sleeves
Creativity
Loneliness
Depression
All heightened
I become nothing
I breathe, that's all I need
No pride and no reason to hide
I contemplate to re-educate
No desire; only a fire
Driven to change
Driven to create
To gain perspective
Yet don't lose compassion
Pursue but don't chase

Love Drunk

With this furious passion came a bottle of wine
The finest wine ever known to man
The flavor of love, the juice of its essence
And at that moment, I took a shot glass
And took my first sip of raw emotion
As time progressed, every good time I had was accompanied
With a drink of this fluid, and I loved it
But time passed, and I stopped pushing the boulder uphill
And took a gulp of love for no reason at all
So it made me drunk
Toxicated with this sensation of compassion
Dizzy with maximum romantic thoughts
And so I fell face foward
Into the concrete of heartbreak
Then I awake to four new emotions, each cruel and evil
Jealousy, lust, hate, and depression
The fourth emotion the most
For now, I'm hungover from past love
Though I still feel it for her
She slipped the poison into my heart
A poison only removed by hard reality
And now, I sit down at the table of innocence
And I take another sip of the fruitful wine
Therefore, this treacherous cycle starts again

War

Wake up upon the early morning
With the enemy already at your throat
With weapons that kill you within seconds
Grab your guns, grab your coat
For you are at war my friend
Smoke and dirt is filling the cold air
Bullets and shells dance in the black clouds
Ash and soot cover your face and your hair
Kiss your families and friends goodbye
The chances of survival are slim
For your enemy will give a big fight
Your foes will try to blow off your every limb
Your old life is behind you
The arms have closed you in
When you're laying there dying
It's a time to count your sin
For you are at war my friend
No one will actually win
This all just started
When one was under an others skin

Barbie Doll

I have heard of the Barbie doll
With her perfect length, strait hair
Her perfect breasts and ass
Her perfect skinny body and tangerine tan
But I've said an important key word here
Perfect!
Since when in the world are things perfect?
Where on this planet do you see a perfect person?
Or perfect anything?
If there is good, then there is evil
If there is a problem, there is a solution
The solution is self-embrace for imperfection
To know that nobody's perfect
And if you think there is perfection
You're stuck in a fairytale my friend
If you truly don't love yourself,
Or your body, or your look
Somebody else does!
Not one person in this world isn't loved
If you think you see perfection somewhere
Then your aren't perfect
And that's okay!
If you look in the mirror and declare yourself ugly and fat
Then the person in the mirror is telling lies!
Perfection is imaginary, You are real

The Medow

A blue, cloudless sky touches the ground in the distance
The grass is a vivid green as it sways
back and forth
The wind is audible, just enough for you to hear
and feel its presence with a soothing cold pet on your cheek
Wildflowers sprout from the ground as if the
dirt had hair strands randomly sticking up out of place
Golden poppies, silky soft dandelions, warm red roses
Trees are off in the horizon
All that surrounds you is an ocean of green
Birds chirp over your head as they teach
their young lings to fly and be free
The sun is not too hot, just enough for
the warmth to counter the gentle breeze
The grass is like feathers tickling your feet
The air so fresh and beautiful
Mushrooms making their presence all around
the earth like it has acne
Then you wake up from this pleasant dream
And sit on your bedside to think
Process the pureness of your fantasy
Then you lay down back to sleep
And dream of your safe haven once again

Human Clay

The human race is made of clay
Everyone is made of it, everyone's changing
The hands of life molds us into new creations
Then bakes us in the oven of no return
But the hands recreate us over and over before that
So they can make us into the ideal creation
So we will be absolutely perfect
But they fail 100%
And when we pass, we are thrown away
Some even forgotten about
In the dumpster of imperfection
Unfortunately, the hands will be interrupted
And will pause in the middle of carving us
So we are put in a foil cocoon to wait
Wait for the hands to work on us again
But why should we wait?
Why wait for someone when we are capable
Capable of ineradicable things that change our world
We should mold our own bodies
Mold our own paths and destinies
Carve the image we want for ourselves
And for others that we love
So don't be baked by the oven of suppression
And become more than human clay

Grey Blood

We all have a dark inferno inside of us
That churns, burns within our once innocent souls
Souls are like sponges for our infernos
They attempt to clean the dirt
And then filter that dirt to different places
But some and most times those sponges
run out of the water of enlightenment
So we can't prevent the growth of the dark
And it hatches
Hatches like a dark, sickening egg
Where shadows of slimy, deadly snake neonate
Make its way out into your system
They slither in your veins, leaving you with grey blood
They sneak to your nerves and bite them constantly
At this time you seem to think all is lost
But the only thing you lost was hope
Your soul still sings about its presence
Your brain is still fighting to live on
And your heart sends the reinforcements
Love, friendship, and trust
I know for a fact that they come in and nuke the system
The snakes evaporate into the air and the
surviving serpents shoot out from your pores
The light flushes the system and don't forget about the light
For it redeems and sews everything back
Don't hurt yourself and stay hurt
There is no need to spill grey blood on the soil of your life

Connecting Dots

The connections that we form
Last for a life time and more
Whether it is good or bad between you
Each of you open new doors
You are only as strong and bold
As the twine that you tie
People come and go as they please
But bonds do not die
As the sun sets in the evening
And the moon takes the sky
Fireflies dance around me like stars
Tears trickle down my eye
Because I have you in my arms
Your head rested upon my shoulder
Such a raw love but tamed like beasts
That make me strong enough to lift boulders
A hug for a hug
A kiss for a kiss
But the days we didn't know each other
Are the ones that I miss
Because when I didn't know you I was lost
But then I was found by you my gentle friend
The days I first met your undying love
Are the ones I want to live again

Lead-Role Intimacy

Do I deserve the feeling she gives me?
The ones dipped in a past coated with darkness but redeemed with night?
Or is it all just something that might?

Do I deserve the praise she gifts me?
The things she smiles at and compliments that hate about myself?
Or is it all just drama I excel?

Do I deserve the way she speaks to me?
The way that makes cloud nine feel like cloud 10
Or am I just being thrown into a lion's den

Do I deserve to be happy with her?
The way I've felt before bet to make something new?
Or am I missing my left shoe?

Do I deserve that joy, well that's my quest
To decide and to let this out of my chest
I want to know more of this better road
But do I deserve to star in my own show?

Masks Fall Down

Blur my eyes from my smiling disguise
Remove my mask
It's glued in place and stuck to my face
I can't get it off
Questioning reality; answering variously
Ignorance is bliss
There is no throne until I get home
Nothing undone until I've won
Longing and waiting
Confusion fading
Need explaining or at least relating
A desire for venting while my heart is renting
In debt from repenting as my existing is dangerous
Because I'll make a change
I'll bring the light; I'll spread the joy even if I fall behind

Neutrality

If I thought and thought
About the black and white rainbow that arks throughout my life
Would I still feel distraught?

If I worked harder and harder
To leave my educational, conceptual prison
Would I still be a martyr?

If I overcame all of the hurdles over and over
Won all the time with anything I do
Would I really be a four leaf clover?

If I erased my mind
And gave away my pain
Would I fall behind?

If I start to love again
To give myself up for temporary feelings
Would I lose my friend?

If I think too long
Sing to many tunes in my head
Would I have sung my last song?

If I thought and thought
About the colorful rainbow ahead of me
Would I still feel distraught?

Under the Bed

My kind is one who needs closure
To avoid exposure, follow the brochure
To feel superior, make others inferior
It's all a part of human nature
But when we don't understand
Or can't and won't comprehend
That's the time we tend
To drive the situation off the deep end
Cause of an idea based on a fable
We shoot any new things off the table
Like new love, new feelings, newly inable
The depressed, the victims, the disabled
Not wanting to listen
Just to discipline
Even something tiny under one's skin
Could be considered a sin
Instead of getting them well
We design them a personal hell
Make the world classify each other as dead
Thus, adding more and more monsters under the bed

Choices of Skyscrapers

The confidence in which I possess
Does not identify who I am
But it does shed light on the degree of what I choose to be
For example, I am a sick human raised by a two headed mutant
But I choose to be the happy, lovable guy that brings smiles
I am the exotic bird on sale in a shady game of poker
But I choose to be the ugly bird who flies free and entertains the other birds
I am the whipping boy who people ventilate their anger on
But I choose to receive the lashes and help them ventilate
You see, who we are is not set
But choices are
Like the foundation of a house
Too much it falls, too little it falls
And that's why we don't know who we are
But we are a hut to start
Just a simple log cabin
Made by our lumberjack lovers
But we can choose
To either shrivel into a cardboard box
Or we can be a skyscraper
And show the sky what we can do

Spellbound

I feel like I've had a spell casted upon me
Every time I say the magic words
I get mad, then sad, then glad it happened
Sparkles absorbed by my pores
Magical dust soaking in
Glow magic man glow!
Bewitched by the obstacles thrown at me
Enchanted by looks given fearlessly
I can hardly tell the difference between haven and hostility
As long as others are there as well
No need for stealth
Shoot a fireball
No need for darkness
Bring your feelings to the light
Wings grown from a crystalized heart
Now you have some as well
Turn me into a toad
Kiss me and I'll be your prince
I'll emerge from the cloud as I bow at your beauty
This is just like of those movies

Home

Swinging trees in a cool autumn breeze
A vivid orange dancing in the wind; straining the sky
Clouds glow to say goodbye to the sun
The world reminding me of its beauty; this must be a dream
Orange cream in the atmosphere above
My environment calms me and reminds me I'm in love
What is love?
Is it admiration, curiosity, infatuation?
Is love only existent when it's reciprocated?
Or am I just asking too many questions?
The heavens have changed the mood
Deep, chill, soothing
The night made its presence and said hello with the sound of singing crickets
The moon made the water shimmer as the lake professed its love with a reflection
Two moons, one above, one below
I desire a third to sit beside me as I become one with the starry maps above
Losing myself in the cosmos while having a comforting, intimate, enchanting anchor to keep
grounded and down to earth
To hold me and run their fingers through my hair while I hold their hand
Then I'll be able to know whatever darkness I may face
Nothing will bring me down, just like the clouds and the moon in the sky
I'll know from the look in her eyes

The Gate

No one deserves to control my life but me
No one tells me what to think
Don't tell me how to breathe
I will always dash back and forth between two worlds in the past
But now that I have two in one
As the wind sings into my ears
I realize that I am okay
As the stars call me home
I now know my name
When the clock strikes twelve
I have to choose a new self
In order to smith the words I need to say, I need time
But time is slipping
Time is dripping
It's drooling, it wants to eat me
I don't think I'm too weak
Just slightly meek
Reflections on the ocean that is my mind
Beneath the water is oodles and oodles of memories
In every single nook and cranny you'll be surrounded with my presence
Welcome to my mind; the vast ocean that is my mind
Come inside, lock the gate on your way in
Don't want the colonizers to come in
That's just a storm waiting to happen

Solution #86

Sunsets only fade with purpose
Stars only come out in the right moments
Violins wail as the wind picks up
As I hear the bow caress the strings slowly, I am brought to tears at
my new understanding of life
Life is the melody
Death is the harmony
Existence is a symphony conducted by all beings
You coexist with each player fluidly while working towards a goal
To invent; to create
Neighbors painting together at twilight
Festivals of chalk coating the ground
Men, women and children dressing up as their inspirations
Crowds of humans dancing, singing, crying, laughing
Fellowships of brothers and sisters all working towards one common goal
How can we stay healthy?
How can we be safe?
How can we be connected?
Acceptance and the willingness to be educated maintains an open mind
Allowing improvement by asking questions
Being welcoming towards all

Trophy Case

Open eyes, the realm of sight
Closed eyes, the dimension of sensation
Don't be limited by your fright
Or you can't expand on your comprehension
Experiment, challenge
Parlament salvage
Caught up in a crossfire of greed and gold
Caught in between a fight over mold
Rabid dogs have more humanity than humans
Smashed fingers between a wooden door and a brass hinge
Blockage due to a lifetime of deprecation
Belittlement as a form of encouragement
Do as we say, not as we do
What we do is not for you
You are not welcome here; but you cannot leave
You are not sick; just ill
We're scared of your potential so take your pills
Gulp them down, are you a zombie yet?
Are you broken yet? Have you given up yet?
Nope! New meds, new pills, you must be saved from yourself
For who you are isn't good enough
You can't sing, you can't learn, you can't find love
You're a creep, you're autistic, you're not what we want
Undesired but if we own you, it's the greatest trophy of them all
So we drug you and polish you
Keeping you in your case

Ill, not sick

Crossed
Alone
Quiet
Isolated
Vibrant energy
Depleting
Color blind
Color there
Trapped
Locked in
Cranium cages
Programming
Destroyed
Yet driven
Question
What now?
One thousand percent
Or zero percent
Choices and decisions
Decide to push and to pull
Empty yet fulfilled
Eye installed
Begin exploration
A cosmic understanding
Only nineteen

Wonderland

A plastic cylinder full of minerals is my ticket out of my creative yet
deepmind
It's not an escape, rather a collection of fine tuned thoughts to educate and
reveal to others that
this is who I am
To understand me, you must listen with an open and intrigued mind
To love me you must understand me
Are you up for the challenge?
The royal you
Some have made it through; some slip through
But all are welcome here
It's an odd place here; rather mad I would say
Yet there is so much beauty in the madness
So much creativity and enriched thoughts in the trees of consciousness
and oceans of
pensiveness
The doors are open; all you have to do is step through
We'll walk in the gardens of my thoughts
We'll lay on the coasts of my imagination
We'll swim in the lakes of my desires
All of this within the dimension of my mind within the crevices of my
hemispheres
Residing in my subconsciousness
Sleeping in my hope
The choice is yours, blue or red pill
Am I the shell you see or more?
The vastness that is my mind hidden within my joyful presence

Corridor

Melancholy hills under a grey horizon
Water droplets echo in an empty hallway
Travel through the door and see a grown man weeping
Someone murdered his wife
Joy was a light, an inspiration and a mother to Hope and Faith
Why would anyone take the life of such a beautiful soul?
Who in their right mind would commit such an atrocity?
Death tears up as he carries this soul upwards
His cloak fluttering in the wind as Joy waves goodbye
The roof parts as ol' grim takes her away
The man's mind bends, breaks, shatters
"Take me!"
"Let me join her!"
"Why?!"
Cries of a desperate human fill the corridor
Wails of a sorrowful souls
Grief, the gift no one wanted
Can't throw it away; can't pass it on
It was tailored for you
Your heart cut in two as the loss consumes you
And he sat there with knife in hand
Hoping to go against the plan
He impaled his blackened heart and it bled
Blood spilled, but he remained still

Greed

Stretched throughout time lies the perfect crime
Discrimination, segregation
The kill order for the human race
Separation leads to dastardly situations
Decolonization is what will push us forward
I hear the tv taunt every day
Mix the ingredients together into a large bowl
Make sure it is well stirred
Then pour the people out into a baking pan
Bake for at least forty-five minutes at four hundred fifty degrees
Don't you see? They are trying to eat us!
They are feeding on our circumstances
Taking our chances; screwing our privileges
Why aren't we getting sick of it?
Why aren't we calling out this shit?
We are continuously put down in submission
Feeding into our temptations
Using us against us
Using our insecurities and weakness to take our money and time
So we're left poor and bankrupt of life
Which propels us into a cycle of earning to live and living to earn
Get money to spend money to get money
Capital greed is more contagious than the flu
Just look at the people
We are playing their games
Playing our minds
I'm done playing games

Invest

You are more than the deprecation you put on yourself
More precious, so loved and admired
From your golden heart to your golden soul
More than enough, anyone would be honored and lucky to have you
When we are in pain, it's hard to see situations clearly
It's hard to look left and right at the same time
When we are in pain, we continuously attempt to do so
So of course it's hard to see what's in front of us
We must allow and allot time to heal through reflection and others
Don't ask yourself questions that are destructive but constructive
One must allow growth
One must accept our past for what it is
Past; no longer present
To learn and overcome is the best escape
And it will allow you to find what you truly desire
Invest in your health, it's worth it

Enigma

If I knew that tomorrow would take me away from you
I'd wish it all away
I'd break all the clocks; smash all the timers
And I'd hold you close
Not as lovers, as dear beloved friends
I'll protect you from tomorrow by immortalizing today
I'll fight through the pain with the hope that I'll see you again
From my fists to my pen, I'll combat whatever negativity that tries to ruin
our frequency
I see two star-crossed souls together on a couch with the lights down;
embracing one another
Comforting each other in the night from their frights
Locking into each other's gaze with a goofy smile on their faces
They created a frequency that changed their worlds forever
A bond that cannot be severed
Love? Maybe
Close friends looking to see where they go? Who knows
All I know is how I feel is the most real thing I've ever felt

Jack and Sally

Driving down a midnight freeway under the moonlit sky
The smell of pines, the sounds of chirping crickets
The night is ours
Road twisting and turning, hands intertwined on the arm rest between us
Hotel California playing softly in the distance
Redwoods pass by as you and I climb the mountain side
Tonight is ours for the taking
Stars, stars everywhere
As far as the eye can see
The moon half full, yet as bright as ever
Lights of civilization in the feet of the hills
Fog migrating over cities below as we float up here
Our conscious and destiny clear
Intent, content, intimate, gazing
Connection with our pupils with an invisible line
Hands and fingers intertwined; locked in place
Then they break and embrace
Eyes not disconnected, nose to nose
Pause to stop time
Your arms wrapped around me
I have joined your side, you've joined mine
"And sit together, now and forever, for it is plain as anyone can see, we're
simply meant to be"

Patience and Sensation

Spine tingling
Face vibrating
Teeth jittering
Saliva gulping
Body vibrating
Head missing
Cloud nine vibes
Toes wiggling
Chest laughing
Heart throbbing
Pounding
Soul complete
Found what was missing
Found what was hiding
Learning, re-learning
Love
Pencil drawing
Patiently waiting
No overthinking
No over reasoning
Logistically speaking
It's all going to work out
Doubt fading
Anxiety slowing
Wounds healing
Depression weakening
Relax, you are okay
Step back and feel
Don't censor, don't run away
Open arms, feel

Heal

Words beneath words
The lines disguise the truths
Yet it's no lie
It's a test to see if you can see what is supposed to be
A test of your ability to know someone's true self
Stop worrying, stop complaining
You will be able accomplish great things if you relax
Just breathe
Don't worry about tests
About any hurdles or hardships
Just worry about your well being and self-love
I do feel, I do understand
No distractions
Just realizations
Insecurities will be gone
Your pain will be minimized
If you just allow yourself to feel
Nothing else
Allow feelings to exist and grow if they want to grow
Peace and love is the key, the final sprint
Driving me to the open door

Healer

I think I've seen you before
I've heard your warming laugh before
Your glistening eyes before
Because everytime you're around me I feel like I'm reminiscing
Like a part life is connecting to me
Saying "you did it! You found her!"
"The woman of your dreams!"
They give me tips
"Be there for her; comfort her"
"Carry her out of the darkness"
You've brought many from darkness to the light
You can do it
Bear the light, be the light
So she can find the light again
A heart in pain is a blind one
Not of choosing, but of the incapability of combating the pain
A blind heart calls for help
I will help you regain sight
If you can't walk I'll carry you
If you can't feel I'll hug the pain away
If you need a shoulder, cry away while I sing to you
Let me in; let me heal you
I am a healer
I won't let you down or be down
You are way too important to me
I'll always bring you light

The ABC's of Fear

All Animals Analyze All Apes
Because Big Buffoons Baffle
Cause Cobras Can Cause Calamity
Don't Do Duties
Feel Ferociously Fearful Friends
Grow Gruesome Green Gods
Hell Horrifically Hollars Hello
I Imagine Ill Ideas, Ideologies
Just Joking, Jump
Killing Klans
Lying Luxuries
Monstrous Monopolies
Never Notice Needs
Overtures Of Obsession
Perpetual People Punished
Quietly Quote Queens
Really Research Report Re-educate
Slowly Show Success
The Tyrant Torn, Tossed
Universal Understanding
Very Viciously Varying
What Worlds We Watch
Yellow, You're Yellow
Zack Zipped Up His Fear

Cupid

How does one absorbed moment become a lifetime of memories in my head?

Why am I certain, so confident?

It is a good thing, don't worry

Your feelings are valid and true

Just take time, allow progression

Patience, she'll come to you

But floating away day by day, wake by wake makes me ponder all the possible mistakes

All the possible impossibilities

Anxiety driven by my desire of understanding

Questioning to me is coping

Or else I'm drowning

Yet I'm also not floating

Just drifting

Deep breath, focus

She does have feelings and you know it

You must be diligent, but relaxed

This will happen when time passes

Maybe not soon, but maybe so

So don't worry, let it happen

No buts, no ands, no ifs

Just let yourself drift

You'll wash up to her shore before you know it

She wants to see you and she's shown it

She cares about you and she said it

She feels for you and it's obvious

So take deep breaths

Be confident but collected

Just do your thing and let cupid be cupid

Anxious Heat

My nerves want to control me
They want me to be home all day and do nothing
To disappear and to vanish
Yet I can't do that, I've come to far
I jutter up and down, left and right
Hands shaking and my heart pounding
The past is trying to creep up on me menacingly
Like I drank one thousand cups of coffee
Calm breath
Vibrations all around me
Peace in warmth
Breathe through heat
Cool down
Relax
Focus on your goals
What are goals?
Milestones in life that you want to reach
Thoughts of a better future yet still grounded in the past
Enjoying the small things
The little joys in life
Remember to live each day a new
To discover and create
To love and assist
To breathe and endure
The best things in life come to those who can balance patience and persistence
Calm breath
Vibrations all around me
Breathe through the heat

Get Up

Fuck the fame
Fuck the wealth
If you aren't in my life
Then fuck it all
If I knew that you'd be driven away
I would have thrown it all away
Even to have just one more day with you
Don't die, I need you
Zack, you are what unites us
You are what completes us
If you pass then we are doomed
If you give up, they die
Pursue your passion
Don't stay in submission
Push forward with full speed
Don't let them break you
The world becomes light soon, I promise
Your pain becomes tolerable, I know it
You'll succeed, I guarantee it
Run
Jump
Climb
Fight
Push
Pull
Break down the walls
Break down the isolation
Break down the pain
Break down the dark
Create light
For the future, for us

Enter the Forest

Rainforests are diameters for harmony
A circle with light as half its radius and darkness another
All I see are flashes of purple, blue, and yellow as I create the conditions of change
Reconstructing from the destruction of Ern
My calltime draws near and I must present my peace
Question, does healing counteract the ideology of fate?
Does health of the mind bring health of the flesh?
Can anyone predict the future under the proper circumstances and conditions?
To feel my love and yours
To contradict my upbringing
To find beauty in pain
Gulping down serums built to charge my quotients
Yet I still feel like I'm missing something
Reaching out to the vault
Reaching for the answers
Searching for conclusion
Disregarding confusion
Don't kiss the cobra, they bite
Unless you welcome death
Don't allow death, welcome it
Death is the beginning of a new life
So we may overcome, adapt
Bitterness, hate, anger
Throw it away
To respark your flame
You must ponder positively and critically

The Barbie

I have heard of the barbie doll
With her perfect length; straight hair
Her perfect breasts and ass
Her skinny body with that tangerine tan
But I have said an important key word
Perfect!
Since when in this world has anything been perfect?
Where on earth have you seen a perfect person?
Or a perfect anything?
If there is good, then there is evil
If there is a problem, there is a solution
The solution is to embrace your imperfections
And to know that no one is perfect
If you think you are perfect, you are stuck in a fairytale my friend
If you truly don't love yourself, or your body or your look
Somebody else does!
Not one person in this world isn't loved
If you think perfection is out there
Then you aren't perfect
If you look in the mirror and declare yourself ugly and fat
Then the person in the mirror is telling LIES
Perfection is imaginary, YOU are real!

The Meadow

A blue, cloudless sky touches the ground in the distance
The grass is a vivid green as it sways back and forth
The wind is audible, just enough for you to hear and feel its presence with
a soothing cold pet on
your cheek
Wildflowers sprout from the ground as if the dirt had hair strands randomly
sticking up and out
of the place
Golden puppies, silky soft dandelions and warm red roses
Trees are off in the horizon
All that surrounds you is an ocean of emerald
Birds chirp over your head as they teach their younglings to fly and be free
The sun is not too hot, just enough for the warmth to counter the gentle
breeze
The grass is like feathers tickling your feet
The air so fresh and beautiful
Mushrooms making their presence all around the earth like it has acne
Then you wake up from this pleasant dream
And you sit on your bedside to think
Process the pureness of your fantasy
Then you lay down
Dow to go back to sleep
And you dream of your safe haven once again
Of your meadow

Bedtime Story

Sleep little one, sleep
Allow your fatigue to take its course
Allow yourself to let go of the day you had
And tomorrow's problems are for tomorrow's you
Lay yourself comfortably in bed with a pillow under your head
Drift away to the atmosphere of your haven
Given thanks for your breath, your joys, your passion
Also give thanks to your pain, obstacles, and sad moments
For dear one, those moments build you up to be stronger, more experienced
Allow growth each and every day
Be kind to your dreams, whatever they may be
Your dreams are just your mind thinking about the stars
Welcome them with open arms
Make sure to put on your favorite jammies
And brush those teeth well
Now rest in bed; lay down your head and dream
Flying hippos on mars in the summer
Aliens playing poker in your palace
A feast fit for royalty your majesty
Drift away
Sleep peacefully little angel
Dream

Dig Deep

I'm a moment captured by fire
A freckle in time that you'll know as a lifetime
So small, yet so impactful to the timeline
Living life, living a small life
But that life is the best life
No worries, no regrets
Traveling down to wonderland
This is my mind; this is me
A true disaster
Bajito, pull the parachute
You only get one chance
God I wish you were here
Now or never
Or the guillotine will have you either way
She, the robot, only wants to talk to me
So let's play hide and seek
Because I fall in love too easily
At least for her, well you, stupid third person
The I am may see odd
But if you stay, I'll melt your worries and pain away
Because just dreaming of you isn't enough
For my heart, I long to conversate, to hug you and gaze into your eyes
You're amazing, caring, beautiful
There are so many pieces of my brain that feel unreal and out of place
All I know is the realest few that I have

Dive

Run, jump, skip
Quick let's dip
Humans are gonna die
Unless your open your eye
Drip drip
Careful don't slip
Blood coast my disguise
I've come to colonize
That's how I used to be
Coding, programming, a means to an end
Now I am awakened and set apart
I'm not immortal or anything
I'm merely enlightened
I found Nirvana
I attacked the core of my pain with questioning
Why I felt that pain
Why should I feel the pain?
How do I break free?
Forgive, allow passage, recover
Phew, I'm okay now
Dancing to the flowers in the sky is wondrous isn't it?
Tis the feeling of love
Up
Up
Up we go
Down, down, down
Going to wonderland

Cottontail

Runaway little rabbit
Run with your tail between your legs
Sprint for your life
Hustle for your existence
I am Mr. Fox
The cunning, sly, mischievous fox
He who feasts
He who dines on your flesh
Flesh, oh flesh
Warm, meaty, moist, red
Mmmmm
The predators, they think this way
They use this mindset to pick us off
To gobble up our legs before they even notice
We the sheep must stand up for our rights
For our freedom; for our passion
In order for us to topple the food chain, we must create a world without
the carnivore
A world without the energy takers
The manipulators and colonizers
We exist too
We feel too
We love too
And now, we strike
We'll take you down
Get over here carnivore

Under the Veil

I feel that feelings feel like the feeling of feels
Crazy right?
Crazy night
Soothing night
Soothingly peaceful night with you under the full moon
Now I'm in the right frequency
Where you can understand me
A place beyond the safety of wonderland
The fourth dimension
I bear gifts, here's your long lost jigsaw piece
I hope it fits just right
Wow, how would you like to die?
What is going to go?
Joy? Sleep? Sanity?
You gotta pick one
You're running out of time
Common man, just choose
Excellent choice
I'll take that off your hands
Now, on with the show
Let go and let me in
Heal

Found

I was stuck in a pocket of self-deprecation
Somewhere in my mind, lost in time and space
Drifting endlessly into my numbers end
On my knees, I wept to anyone who could hear me
To someone out there
Then you found me
You saw me trapped in my cave and brought me to wonderland
Then from wonderland, I unlocked my potential
I found myself in myself
All thanks to that light
And I was saved
Ripping the chains off my mody and switching on my mind
I found the ability to say hi
Your stare met mine
And we exchanged names
Time progressed
Feelings manifest
My heart beating so fast it broke through my chest
I didn't know where it went
Poof, just gone
I walked so lonely for so long
Then you walked in again with my missing piece
I found my angel

Hour Hand

Buckle up my sweet child
We are about to go for the ride of a lifetime
Down the road we go
Letting ourselves leave everything we know
Just you, me, and the land of the free
A paradise in a sick dream
Lines in the road are lines in reality
What is real? Was it figmented?
What am I to do to show you the truth?
Phantoms chase us as the wind increases
They soar in the clouded sky; welcoming the thunder
Then the thunder summons the rain
All the sudden, I see lights in my eyes
I found the infection in my brain
I bleed and I cry
To drive out what makes me insane
Bury me if I lose
Find me when I disappear
Seek me if I'm no longer here
I'm just hidden, not gone
Not forgotten
Search
Pursue
Discover me

Winter

The vivid Autumn leaves slowly drift their way to the earth in tranquility
Dancing in the wind as they lay to rest
Accepting their final resting places as home
Orange, yellow, and red exhilarating and vibrant colors paint the ground
One one condition
That the winter comes, that the cold surfaces once again
The cool, chilling season of new death and inevitable life
A time for reflection
As if you looked in a mirror of ice and didn't recognize your face
Then you learned every winkle; every crevice
Your body numb
Your mind numb
As you reach for the sun
Where did you go?
Who am I?
How did I get here?
Questions
Responses hidden in small specks of time and space
Pondering the conditioning of the human race
Seasons are reasons to change
Drop your dead leaves
Rebuild your bark
Grow upwards to the sky
Then, and only then
Spring will come

True Gold

True intimacy is something I've never experienced before
Not just a crush, not just infatuation or care
Love. Real, exhilarating and connecting love
The feeling of my heart begging to burst out of my chest
The sensation of an embrace that is capable of stopping time
The rush of fingers from my beloved slowly petting my arm and hair
True, deep, unworldly love
Roses on your birthday
Christmas spent wrapped in blankets and clinking mugs of peppermint
cocoa
Halloween couple costumes as we trick or treat
Intertwined on the couch and watching movie after movie until we fall
asleep
Snuggled up and warm
Gazing into your lunar eyes, spellbound and bewildered by your genuine
and warm smile
I am so, so blessed and overjoyed to have you in my life
I can see myself clearer
I can breathe better
Climb faster, jump higher
I even have my fingernails back
So thank you for banishing my deprocation
Thank you for your love and care
Thank you for being you
I am so gifted and so honored that I have you in my life
You glitter more than gold

Primitive

Swing, swing little monkey
Soar in the trees
Feel the autumn breeze
Wind is in your hair; traveling without a care
What's that? That over there?
It's a big, vicious cat! Don't get scared!
Just swing on, you're no pawn
Just an ape searching for meaning
Just a human meaning to search
Cousins and relatives
Government fugitives
Your culture? Mine!
Your language? Mine!
Your choice? Our choices!
Bang your drums and beat your chests
Time for revolution and time for change
Freedom
Liberation
Or extinction
Your discretion and your decision

Crossed

Pass the blunt; pass my pain
Spinning in circles until I see you again
Questioning reality
Reality is questioning
Doubt is a calamity
But overthinking causes diminishing
Floating abyss
How'd it come to this?
Death is romanticized in the vision of suffering eyes
Embrace the agony of your history in order to heal fully
Find light in the smaller things
Baby steps
Find meaning in connections
Toddler steps
Create meaning in bonds you forged
Child walking
Feel the deeper emotion of our growing link
Teenage running
Embrace relaxation through me and I shall do the same
Embrace that we are connected
Realize our new reality and just stop questioning
Stop over analyzing
Look at her actions; her words
What does it reflect?
Care, admiration, intimacy, compassion, respect
Love?

Caisson

Sleep? What is sleep?
Is it the absence of filters?
The act of refreshing our energy?
The bringer, gifter of peace?
I don't know anymore, it's been too long
So long since the fear started to take over
Now I dread sleep
To sleep is to be in solitude with my horrors
But insomnia is isolation
Pick your poison
Reliving your most antagonizing, dreadful, torturing moments
Or feel so utterly alone that you lose your ability to hold back tears
PTSD
A scar on your left arm
A crystal ball shattered on the floor, then glued back together
Dancing with one leg
Singing with no voice
Seeing without your right eye
The last component to the equation of Skips
Thing one, thing two
Who is thing three?
Does that exist?
Harmony? Tranquility?
Whatever the answer is, I am so close
So close to shattering the mirror

Aces Low

I've dealt with the felt material you made my sweater with
The shame that you wanted me to hold with each individual stitch
The discomfort you made me feel inside every single day
You should not sing
You are incapable
You fucked up
Every interaction came with an unequal consequence
My existence never made any sense
Was told by peers, friends, teachers that I was a unique light
Then I came home and I wasn't your perfect son
I'm sorry
Sorry I'm not what you asked for
That I replaced a suit and tie with rings
That I can't be sick with you
You live in an imaginary world where you can never be wrong
A place where my dad is non-existent and treated as a hostile
I'm not yours, I know the truth
You don't deal in truths
I fold my hand; goodbye
Take the money, I'll take my life back

Rebirth

Lost
Lost, then found
Found by you here in this haven
I'm finally safe
Fear
Fear dissolving away
Threw them out the window
I'm finally okay
Death
I was dead
Found the next chapter
Gonna life another day
Paths
All roads lead
They lead to my peace
I've never felt this way
Building better buildings
Feeling, I'm finally feeling
Thanking myself for everything
So joyful, I'm crying
I have ignited my dead heart

Peep Hole

Heaven can't welcome me yet
I can't stop now, not when I'm this close
I am so, so close
The taste is so vivid
The smell is so rich
Plant my legs in concrete so that I can break through them
Throw me in the ocean to drown so I can come back from the dead
I'm a zombie if that's what you perceive
Can't die until I see the end
Can't leave until I know what happens when I stay
Beneath the sea; I rise
I am four Earths high
Eleven dimensions long
Nineteen aura's deep
If only I would leave it all behind
If only I could see into your mind
Would leave it all behind
If only you saw my kind
Then I would drive to find
Scholar
Brother
Lover
Bearer
Savior
De-colonizer
Uniter
Your best friend all the way to the end

The Door

The glossed, dark hazelnut entrance beholden many intriguing questions
The grains of the wood still visible beneath a hard yet smooth shell
Fingers slowly coo the door's center as I find the knob
A brass covered hinge to keyhole with the prints of those who have attempted to enter
Grasping, turning, opening, gasping
Behold! Oh what a sight this is!
Spinning greens bearing delectable and scrumptious fruits
Wavey blues that welcomed home many flying monster fish
Yellow rays of hope, compassion, and joy hug my chilled nose
Met with the glow of a full moon, refilling the will to live for a little while longer
All on a night's sky similar to the one we first met
Realization strikes my spiral nerve, sending me a lethargic jolt from my head to my toe
Confidence meets bewilderment and my thoughts are cleared
This is a world we built together
A perspective we both fueled and empowered to exist
I care so much about you
And you really care about me too
Simply put, I'm no longer afraid and I love you

Checkers

The gruesome presence of a slimey, grotesque mother towers over young
two hits
Nose flaring like a bull and red eyes to match it
Her crooked smile intensified as she began to speak
That voice still haunts me to this day
"Why?"
"Why are you not sick?"
"I'm sick, so you must be too!"
Suddenly, the young lad was lifted by collar and was dragged to the iron
chair
"Buckle up, here we go!" she screamed
A spoon raised over head along with my impending dread
I close my eyes and say my prayers
Urk!
Spoonfed the lies
Gag!
Force fed the pain
Gulp!
Never will be free again
Blindfolded and strapped in a rusted chair
Lifeless, famished and parched
Pale, oh so pale
My mouth gaping open to a new understanding
I am not dead
Yet
I am not sick
Anymore
I'm struggling to break my body free
Doing the next best thing
Holding my breath to prepare
Soul escaping my fresh-bound circumstances

One Armed

Doomed with despair
Feeling hopeless
Feeling alone
Depression meets agony
Tragedy after tragedy
My reality is searching for strength
Desiring the courage to inclitation
I don't even know, I just feel anxious
Head is brain dead but I'm not giving up
I'm not giving in
But it's hard when no one sees the pain I'm in
Encased in this drowning sensation
Yet I'm above water watching myself drown
Save him!
Someone dive in! He's dying!
With a poof, he was gone
Not under or above water
Just gone; none-existent
Where did he go?
Nobody knows

Skin Me

Skin me
Take my skin and display my shell for all to see
Let them either stand in horror or understand who I am
What I've been through
What I've endured
Stuff me
Make me a taxidermy daydream
Put the body in your den to accompany you while you sip your wine
You must want me to die
You must like that I'm blind
I have no eyes anymore
Sell me
Bag over my face, I'll serve the highest bidder
No need to pursue if you don't contribute
Why lecture when you can support?
Why support when you can kick my corpse?
Kick, after kick, after kick
Down for the count
Yet you're still beating me
I don't need you to fix me
Just listen to me
Don't you understand that I had to rewire my whole mind?
Don't you understand I don't have the luxury you had?
Sanity

Comfort

It's time to choose
Detach or strive
Push or be pulled
Will you choose wisely?
To keep your love
Remember you are enough
Please don't give up
I need you in my life Zack
I can't do this without you
You need me, I need you
A heart of gold; a warm aura
Zack you'll change the world
Shhh, hey
I will always be by your side
Don't forget, never forget
I love you
My choice has been made
I'll push to cope with the pain
Even in the acid rain
You'll stay the same
Take my hand and walk away from the knife
Throw away the pills, it's not your time
Please don't die on me
I can't lose you

Premonition

Gazing at the night sky through the bottom corner of your couch
God what a night
God what a girl
I feel the discernment of quietude vitally for the first time in a long time
Joyful, fulfilled, safe
I feel
Safe
Even in this warzone
A fight fought on three planes
North, South, and present
Centered between a conflict built on greed and hate
On my knees
Broken hands and broken legs
The loon wants to take me hostage while the other whips insecurities
Inches away from death
Abruptly, an angel swooped from the sky and soared me onward
Away from this dreadful place
To this day I am still healing and processing those imprinted horrors
Yet I feel so comfortable in my leather
Finally I can believe in the current
Opportunities are utterly incredible, amazing and beautiful
Golden heart and a soul brighter than the sun
Your mind more gorgeous than anything I've ever known
I wish I could give you the world

December

Stripes, lines and designs collide and confined in my wavelength mind
Rose as red as my blood
Fill the cup with wine and light the candle made of mud
Leave the poison behind
Ladders lead to paradise; I throw my hands to the sky
Floating and singing octopi
We welcome you home; we're glad you're home
Home is with us
Home is in us
Mono to stereo
Conversation to radio
Who really knows this face?
Who has explored the cracks?
The wrinkles, crevices and lips?
Hello dear reader, I hope you comprehend
What it's like to feel the benz
Impounding one's trauma like a sledgehammer to the skull
Filling them with ghastly, dark water
CPR! This man needs attention!
Get an MRI stat!
Why is he dying?
It's like his brain is on fire!
No, God no!

Ghost

The rain poured down, grey skies wept
Beloved standing before my grave
Weeping on her knees
Screaming for my return
Transparent and invisible, I can only cry from my mirror
Every word I hollar and not one taken in
She can't hear me, I'm not alive anymore
Thunder's somber purrs sedate me
Anxiety timed to the flashes of sporadic electricity
Seeing her crumble and breakdown before my name
I'd sell my soul for just one more second
Please, just one more
Give me my arms so I can hold her tight
GIve me my chest so she can hear I still beat
Just give me a voice so I can tell her I love her
Let me fucking live again
Chained to my casket; yanking the metal does not bend or break it
Trapped in an eternity where I watch you suffer forever in loop
Closed eyes only make known the weeping
Immersed in your audible throat gasping for air in between wails
Opened eyes force me to see your destruction
What can I do but watch?
Nothing
Letting go of the chains
Placing these freezing hands in my stone lap
I shed a lifetime of tears as I howl
Two souls cursed by the grave

Drill Sergeant

Bring forth the blade of truth
It shall sever the lies form my mind
Pondering, questioning
Spiraling
Not powerful enough to be rid this pain
Finding meaning causes headaches
Drilling sensations into tense temples
Grinding my grey matter
These legs won't stop shaking
I keep baking and baking
Addiction, my savior and destroyer
High to detach
Lit to fade
Cannabis for the pain
I know it's not good, but I want to sleep
I know I'm dying and I do want to live
Show me a path instead of your wrath
Something that's able to be traveled independently
Give your support, not your whip
I shut off your pointless lectures
I know the problems and I need the solutions
Better yet, just hold me as I weep
I want to sleep

Trial

The tree sways ominously in the wind
Leaves crinkle beneath excited feet
Mr. Prosecuted is silent before the violent executioner
Knotting the rope in front of his masked face
The crowd was struck by a curious horror as the mayor spoke
"Treason! He fed the poor! He helped others and gave his life for the greater
good! There is no
greater good than me!"
For this, he was to be hung by the neck until death
A blurred vision of the crowd stained Mr. P's corneas as he uttered his
final address
The woman he loved in the crowd; breaking down
Hairs from the slip tickled his clavicle as the rope embraced his neck
Deep breath in, deep breath out
This is his end

Cogs

Spin around another time
Why don't you speak your mind
Is it really hard to find all the quills on a porcupine?
Did you ever truly see the inquired memories?
Hold me, don't choke me
Cradling a soul is so hard when you're but a simple bard
Filled with the longing to be a star
Though I'd be depressed from being so far away
Stop! Why did you proceed?
Making your way to my radar as you bolt
Dancing on a hike as I embrace the trail of spikes
Really wish I had a bike
Secrets intrigue me, yet I can't know them yet
You're not synced correctly time traveler
Cease the search for answers
Cosmos gift desires if you stop getting wired
Become the wait
If it's fate, it's fate
You know the gate and you know the heart
The missing part

Below

The night was young and chilled, boasting as it danced
Shivering as the walk is wearisomely blase
Nothing but stretched out, cracked sidewalks as far as the eye could see
Concrete subtly beneath the avenue of streetlights
Jacket rips expose irritated skin
Cold tattooing my arms with red and purple
Grinding my teeth as air clouds escape warm breath
So, so many homes surround me and not one is my own
Exhausted and incompetent kneecaps kiss the pavement as I surrender to gravity
Crick, crack, crunch
The road falls beneath me and I look to my left as I am about to meet the abyss
My home screams as it reaches out a desperate hand
"Don't go! Please don't do!"
"Don't take him from me!"
I couldn't harbor anyone else
"Goodbye my dear"
Final words of the final light
The road beneath me fully caves in and I plummet infinitely into oblivion
Her screams emanate my ears as I plummet
No escape, no death
Forever imprisoned

Above

"Hello" said the floating, crooked grin
"I am Dentalgon, protector of the teeth"
"I will be your tour guide into paradise"
Shocked as I scanned my surroundings
No walls
No floor
No roof
Space, space as far as the eye can see
A beautiful nothingness amongst ridiculously sized light bulbs
Bobbing up and down as my body tickles as if I were underwater
Eyes wide open, deep beneath the sea
Air bubbles escaping my mouth as I lose my oxygen
Slowly my lungs shut down but still I seem to breathe
Bewildered and reaching for my neck
Gils! I have gils!
Scales! I have scales!
I swim in circles; I swim with glee
I am a fish you see!
Abruptly, I hear a growl behind me
Body shifting
Blood runs cold
Slowly turning to face a black and grey striped shark with blood thirsty, red eyes
I have no time to scream as it shreds me in two
Head and body separated as he gobbles the conscious half and swims onward
Hello, I'm Skips
I'm a head that lives in a fish

Chesh Pink

As I lay barren on a sea of green
I am surprised by the smell of bagels
Warm, soft bagels on a Tuesday
The color yellow tinting my eyesight
Laughter, joy, contentment
Sit back and enjoy the show you goons
I am a grey cat on a dirty carpet
A pretzel falling to the floor and a crunch from the bread
The combination of yellow and purple now pink and red
All of them rumbling within my head
A cheshire cat in the touch of my leg
Making his way to get the waffles
It can't be like this forever
Something will give
Unless
Unless you develop your patience, your independence
Relax, you'll be okay sesame seed
You'll be just fine
Let's travel time
Have a blast
Don't look to the past
Experience to find your haven
Doesn't it make sense?
You can fly; you can soar
You are adored
Flying cheshire cat

Zion

The moon was full in the kingdom of Nod
Lighting the valley in the utmost beautiful way
It was an enchanting sight indeed; a sea of oak
Trees painted by a lunar gloss coat zephyr
Just as if you were looking in a photo lost in time
Forgetting the most beautiful sight to sapian kind
The kingdom was not one of riches, or kings, or luxury
Rather a small community of houses around an old, photonic brick castle
Citizens of all creeds and fashions living together in tranquility and treaty
A concord between the desire to need and the need to desire
Balancing the fragile relationship of love and power
Sky split in two, day sun and night moon
As if a painter got confused mid-way into the canvas
Puzzled by their own creation
This place, like no other than I've seen before
I've fought for my world to be centralized around peace
Yet this world has everything
So much understanding
Unconditional love
Can this kingdom come here?
Can it exist in this plane? This realm?
Hopefully
I long to show you all this place
Though I shouldn't yet
You see, you must open your hearts and your minds to the posabilities
To the probabilities
To the communities
This could be our world

3.0

Accomplishments come with a cost
If you get what you've been searching for, you might lose your eyes
What is the point of this pencil? This book?
Personal suffering renders beauty to others
Fulfillment risks the loss of flow
Artists create from the deepest parts of their pain
What happens when you take mine away?
Will you and I see each other one day?
My head is full of mucus; sick from confliction
Someone comfort my curiosity with abrasiveness
I need a medal of courage and I'm not lion
Trembling cells from a previous love
Should I love again?
What do I have to lose?
Maybe the information would cause growth
9:00AM
Time to face the screen
Time to accept my failures
Time to move forward
Accept the call
Don't let them talk shit
Open wide or time to die
Kill the tick
Murder the anxt
Behead the buffoon
Become the next version of you

The Moon's Lament

An old, wooden swing drifts apathetically in the eerie breeze
The vibrational frequency of murder aimlessly filling souls with dread
"Who?" Screeches the concerned owl as if to forward a mysterious presence
Look beyond the bewitched trees
Fireflies perform the dance of death
Danse Macabre wails from their motion
Notice their gemini jurisdictions
Light and dark raise those who have been forgotten
A hand penetrates the infertile soil
Then a torso, then a leg
The grave of the lightest man violated by the resurrected
"Why did I return to the land of the living?"
"Who is summoned my soul?"
With movements swiftly inhuman, a hooded figure entered stage left with
a bouquet of black
roses
To the surprise of the shambled corpse, a woman's familiar voice caressed
his rotting lobes
"Welcome home angel"
Unveiled, the love of his life slowly approached him
Reaching out her hand for him to take
Woefully yet joyfully, he took her hand into his own skeletal grasp
A smile cracked the reanimated face of her lover as she shedded her grief
with tears
They embraced each other under the light of the full moon; reunited and
re-discovered

Shhh, they hear

Silence is the only friend I've been able to rely on since the solitude began
It's the only peace that remains in a world singed by humanity
The sun died long ago, yet the world is still warm from the piled mounds
of the deceased
This was a trial no one could foretell
Atmospheric and cosmic destruction
A trial by fire with no flame
Humanity crumbled before the positron virus
What would you do if you could achieve your darkest desires?
What would you do if your father stood before you with a jagged grin and
a cleaver in hand?
Would you gag from the blood drenched streets?
I carry the last remaining torch on the globe
The last light, pure and warm
A moth's dream coated in ecstasy
Pitter patter
Drip drop
Heavy breathing
The noises of the void ring my ears, causing me to abandon sanity
Ripped hands shake my head as I attempt to drive out the temptation of
the darkness
Solitude is maddening, yet so is intimacy
I haven't seen another human in many, many years
Hope is just not enough anymore
I lie to myself to stay alive
Don't worry, it will be okay fireman

Sweet Dreams

Alone, destructed, afraid
I lay on my alter, gazing at my distractions
Colors soothe me such as a mother's lullaby
It's time to say goodbye
The flesh dominates the embodiment of my aura
Beginning to lose its pulse
Each integer accumulated in my BPM is slowly stripped from my heart
Down, down, down
Falling endlessly
Spiraling clockwise to the final tick
Breathe in, breathe out
Deeply and serenely
Time to say your final goodnight
You'll be forgotten just as the branches that led to you have been
Alone in life as in death itself
So why not welcome a new beginning?
Flem slowly fills my esophagus to the brim
Breathing decreases
Boom boom, boom boom, boom boom
Organs shut down as bile packs for a vacation
Boom boom, boom boom
My eyes bulge as I fight for even a millisecond longer
Boom boom
Fluids line up at the gate, ready to depart
Boom
Everything is released from my stomach
Parading in my mouth as it suffocates me in my sleep
I am too tired to fight it
Drowning in shame as I say goodnight

Roulette

Spin the forty-four again
Let's dance with fate again
One in the chamber
One ticket to the maker
Who will be blessed with their end?
Five enemies and one friend
The baker
The playwright
The dancer
The philosopher
The doctor
The best man
Perspective in motion
Past the terror quotient
Round and round and round again
No end, no end, no end
Dizzy from watching and waiting
Pondering who's waltzing with dying
Tonight, tonight
Like molasses, the revolver slows, ceasing its first kisser
All wide and bulging eyes dart to the doctor
He gulps in reaction to the intensity
Killing the healer could be the perfect conspiracy
Grasping the handle, sweat drenching unclean pores on his face
Struggling to keep down lunch as he lifts the weighted barrel painstakingly
towards his mouth
The metal becomes lodged in his lips as he tightly shuts his eyes
Dug fingernails in palm, drawing blood
The silence deafening
Click

The Prison That Is My Mind

Nothing seemed to be alive within the dark-lit room

Somehow still serene beneath the Earthly crest

A blood-curdling scream from a panicked, tortured woman bombards every surface of the

present environment

Why doesn't she focus her pupils?

Where are her eyes?

A plasma drenched spoon calmly sits on a silver platter painted by a green tint from the lights

Hostage, the woman is now one with the agony

An iron angel lost in time

Nails ripped off her cracked fingers and missing toes

And still she won't cave in

Still won't give up the secret of life

Why? Why is she so attached to the question as old as the universe?

A riddle built to imprison any unfortunate being who dared to attempt to solve it?

An enigma disguised as an innocent, intriguing puzzle piece

The one tied around her battered neck, resting on her gashed chest

Determined and driven for an answer

Dependent and addicted to the hope of a response

She can leave anytime she wants, the straps are unlocked

Why does she stay?

No one else has tried to pick this brain

She must also be insane

I'm here to take her place

Attention, about face!

Paging Dr. Misery

The sun is trapped in a gun
Bullet cased in star blood
Itchy trigger on shaking finger
Someone shot the clouds

Mudurer, you killed the heat
Traveler, you broke your feet
Animal yet cannibal's see your edible
Please let me out

Caged, enraged, I fight
Die alone? I might
Clipped my wings, no flight
Think I'm scared? You're right

Toxic shadow in mellow sick
Toothpicks for a fellow controlled by ticking and tocking
Clock broken yet woken within a dream
Joy and pleasure hidden within the cream
Rosebud gone
Cherry said farewell
Tapping my fingers to the table as I wait
Depressed into a blank, busy room
Restless and deprived of comfort
Waiting to see the world again
I'm called, allowed in
Who am I? Family friend
Rushing in by his bed
Comatose but not dead
Maybe

Control, Release

The individual grains of pouring sand rush through the hourglass
Gravity claiming each and every second of my remaining time
Each mineral creating a pile of reminding moments locked in time
Seconds become minutes
I don't have much left
Minutes created hours
But you'll remember for years
All it takes is a couple of seconds to generate a lifetime of fears
If time were a person, they'd be old and shrew
Even though they'd be seen as evil and cruel, nothing would compare to their care
Take the stretched hand of time
Take comfort in the lack of control
Stop trying to control your desires
Be an eagle that soars through the timeline
Be free
Be elated for the opportunity to improve your circumstances
Open your mind; open your heart
Find peace in time
Time for peace
Let go

Frozen

Floating away aimlessly down an icy stream
Clouds of heat escape my lips
No warmth here, how'd it come to this?

Lost my loose mind in a place I cannot find
My face freezes over as I long for a hand on my cheek
The arctic depression crushes me like a boulder

Frost bites me in every fiber, every inch
All I feel is little tingles and pinches
No journey, no destination as I drown in expectations

Blast this shivering cold
I have no clothes and flesh ensnared in ice
Sold, these lifeless grey eyes are no longer bold

Hopeless
Dead
Loveless
So full of regret
Stretched arms
Empty head
Sorrowful freeze as I make my way down stream

SoS

Hello? Are you there?
This is passion, I'm scared
There's a darkness outside
I have nowhere to hide
Send help, please!
This is no joke or tease
It's trying to break in
It wants my shell of skin
It's come before but it wants more
Bring help, there's no protection here!
Please hold dear
All of our officers are out of town
Sorry we let you down
And just like that, the line went dead
Passion became trapped within a dying head
The darkness kept pounding
Door starts crumbling
She uttered her goodbyes
Then the void got inside
To this day, we don't know if she's still alive
Anyone who says this is fake is telling you a lie
Be serious, not delirious
The world will grow grim if we do not do our part
Find love and peace or else we are all dead
Imprisoned within our head

End Game

"Hello" screeched the vultures in the melancholy, grey sky
Pulses of light surface from the dirty cotton balls above
Rain bombards the ground with grace
Hydrating and washing the blood from his face
The heavens cry as flesh slowly fails its host
Thousands of soldiers surround their captain with silence
Showing respect as they take a knee in the thick mud
His comrades know he doesn't have much time
In the distance is Mara, the god of darkness
Cut deeply and quartered; defeated
But to kill him, he had to be willing to sacrifice the one thing he needed
to live
Himself
For the good of mankind, he gave his life
Choosing a tragic passing to open new roads in the timeline
How could one man create such a large web?
How did he connect the masses?
Who is he?
Eyes slowly start to close with tranquility
A smile cracked the battered face of light
His last words, uttered into the ear of Dohoro
"She has the potential to replace me"

Forcast

Hello, I am the weatherman
I can tell you about the clouds
Let's spin around the map again
Make sure to bring your coat
Today is gonna be impassiveness with a touch of hail
Don't worry, you won't mold as long as you stay out of the moat
Winds will zoom from the north while the rain travels west
March your boots henceforth; grab your iron coats
Progress and success are not lies in your chest
Make sure to try your best
You'll find inside I cry
Steady eyes devise so embrace my device
Cherish my ice while you're shivering in Anvi
Who's your shield now?

Contrast

Three as you can see defines the formaic puzzle
Meshing into the golden afternoon in this mysterious place
Where trees are made up of codes of twos and zeros
Bushes sprouting leaves made of ones and sixes
Mathematical concoctions slice errors on my skin
Pushing the objective of the fifth dimension
Pain is now present in this place
Existence as we know it is designed in a numeric fashion
Small yet influential variables of a cosmic equation
Open wide, time to be heard
Speaking firmly to the problems will create drive for a solution
No one wants to accommodate when they're consumed with confusion
Conditioning is the generational chip implanted in your mandula
They want you so desperately yet you hold the power
Rush down the waterfall and meet the lake with a kiss
Destruction of westernization creates tension for those who swirl their wine from afar
No such goods exist in the lives of the common folk
To take a step towards equality
We must provide truth educationally
Slice their desires into quartered compromises
Past events, the moment before, they have floated down the stream
Time to open the gift in front of us

Rabbit Hole

Down, down, down
Down the hole we go
Drifting to a new, bold place
An existence I've never known
Endlessly, curiously observing the anomalies
Birds with no wings
Cats with no whiskers
Dogs with no bark
Clocks with no face
Curious, curious things
My depiction of this realization is conflicting
Everything fathomable escapes
If I didn't know better, I'd say I've been trapped in translucent form
A phantom as I continue to descend
The cosmic question of personal existence become checkers branded on
my cones
The wise men sit down to play; I wager your resignation
I'll bring my gifts, let's see who breaks
Go on, you make the first move
I've planned the whole game
Predicted every move
How could you possibly win?
Confidence
Persistence
Endurance
And realizing I already won

Thread

The pieces fade into the endless void
Slowly creating an endless, empty gap in this dimensional place
Each fragment of influx continuum gradually bringing a sense of intriguing
dead
How the fuck are we not dead?
Imagine as if there was a hole in your eyesight
Right in the corner of your eyes; your peripheral gaze
Clones can look left when you look right
Yet focusing forward welcomes the destruction of tunnel vision
Almost as if you never lost the ability to see in the first place
The whiteness is blinding
Squint your glass globes or your pupils will corrode
Close the rip in the timeline by not focusing on the rip
Forcing and imposing will create two more slashes along side the initial
gash
Find your needle hidden in your sea of worth
The thread lies in knowing love and connecting to others
With care, sew what we reaped when we started this war
Only then will the sun bear it's shine once more
Complete the puzzle

Shine

Show me the moon and I'll bring the stars
Dancing in candlelight as long as I am where you are
The scent of wax and the warmth from your hand
Lit by a distance screen, no place better in the land
Take me in and seal my skin
Show my heart that love can begin
Let me in
Allow me to heal
I'll show your heart that this is real
How we both feel
Touch communicates intentions
Insecurity allows pretension
Feel the positive tension between us and we'll bring down the walls
We'll shatter them with one blow from the light we emanate
We'll bring them warmth, you and I
With the gold inside

White is Blank

White is the mind who chooses to stay uneducated
Ignorance transforms into arrogance, inviting the teachings of colonizers
Unwilling to comprehend and understand outside cultures, practices, and
perspectives
An inability to process and learn new teachings and lessons
Blank in mind and taste
Unable to think original, uncredited thoughts and questions
Colonization imprisonment on a mental level
Just as the black and white grain on a disconnected television
Whiteness is taught and handed down then retained due to an inadequate
and narrowly selective
education
To be rid and cure the minds, we must rebuild and re-educate
Hate will only fuel and feed the initial, blind loathing they were taught
Whiteness is not a skin color, it's a mindset
Flesh is not your potential ally rather the minds of those who cannot escape
their washing
Hating someone for their ignorance is equally unhelpful and destructive
Teach them, decolonize them
Bring them culture, human culture

Endless

Look to the sky for crystal eyes
Levitating, shimmering distonance
Ruby pupils with an emerald iris
So long planet Earth, goodbye
I'm alone here in the atmosphere
None of my friends can fly
Floating in zero gravity while constantly decoding
Solitude consuming me while watching a blue sphere corrode
You so desperately want to die, but why?
If we all focus on improving there's no winning or losing
Neutrality isn't a curse, nor is the life you live
Please don't kill yourself like the other kids
You can't believe in love, and I cannot let you give up
This is all the strength I have and I still don't feel enough
So maybe I'll just take your place
Harbor your agony so you can see your face
I love you dear human; I believe you can do it
Now believe that you'll live
If you want peace, you gotta give

Scythe

Set in stone is the grim call of fate
Knocking firmly on the skeletal gate
Mind solidified, not up for debate
Only a matter of time
A blessing, a curse
Wishing you the best at my worst
Throat burned by bile, unquenchable thirst
Unacceptable hippocampus burst
There is healing in death
There are lies beneath the threat
No cause to the affect
Do you hear the nonsensical, indistinguishable derelict?
Goodbye angel
May we dance again
Goodbye beautiful
Soon I'll be dead
The man the world loved never seemed to be enough
The reaper arrives with his silver blade

Travesty

It's just another day in no-dreamville
The sun tucked away by the smog
The moon kidnapped by the grey
Solitude, thy name is depression
No more expression as the baby sleeps indefinitely
Tainting the parents endlessly
Friends? Carelessly non-existent
Fuck persistence
Momma picked up the dead bun
"I'll miss you hun"
Chucked the body out the window as she clapped away the dirt
Called her hubby with a flirt
"Let's make another one, or let's make a widow"
Snuffed out pop late last night with a pillow
She cried and cried through gouged out eyes
His final mark
No one believed her bollshit, she was sent to prison real quick
So there you have it
Two deaths and old habits
"Dead rabbits" croaked the frog; ribbit
Fuck the heart, rip it
Dad and I are non-existent
Momma's the only one alive as we're deceased inside
Wish I could hide

Tucked Away

What is the point of anything when the pen loses its numbing?
All the cracked roads to Rome destroyed
Time to look towards the wooden boy
Sawdust tears, glass bead eyes
Velvet clothes and a brass wind
Sitting on the distant shelf
No brain, heart or wealth
I'll let you down again
So keep me up there friend
Marionette strings bind me as I watch you leave silently
Who were you? Where were you?
Who am I? What am I?
Click clack, no turning back
This is the call, the death of Zack
Screech to a halt
No one's fault
I am doomed
Tonguru
Thank you for my peace

Amnesia

I dream of a day you'll come home to me
Embrace the light and ease your pain
Insecurities to burn; depression to break
Sense the heat, it's time to learn
Cattywampus lines in place
Reality is split as questions encourage continuum
Clocks with no faces
Twisted trees in gentle breezes of paradise
Death's brilliance, a true gem crystalized
Caught up in my head amongst all the petty lies
Oh won't we give up the need to perceive?
Little mice in time
Swim on forward
Sprint towards your goal
Reach the stars from the depths
I'll soon be where you are
Luna dear, don't you fear
I am here a little longer
We still have time

Overture

Darkness has befriended me where the waters have consumed me
I have failed to see the light coming from the blight above
The sun's rays painfully corrode emotions, giving back what I a owed
The right path was never one I was showed
So I destined to fall down
My blood is black as I no longer can go back
The revolution is on the attack
My battle cry brings many frowns
My drive is pure
It's my cure
This is the overture
Time to escape the ground

Lazy

The wind coos just one more time
Penny for thoughts? I'd pay a dime
Well if it isn't the rooster!
Trotting down the road again with no family or friends
Well now I gotta catch a booster
No nut redemption
Dark temptations
I vanish
Accept your fate your clever plate
You ran away with the spoon
Brother I am sorry I can't go to your party
Lethargic
Apathetic
I don't wanna finish this poem
I'm fucking lazy

Weak

Grateful for the freckle in time when I was able to sit by your side
I want to be there with you eternally so I may be bewitched by your eyes
once more
Interlocking our chilled fingers with your rested head on my shoulder
Will I never see you again?
I feel my faint heart growing colder
You are supposedly here but not present
The distance is unpleasant
Each time we speak I ask, and I try, but I'm too weak
And I can't handle your absence
You can't handle, well I don't know
Is there something to build? May I please see it grow?
If you are going to shoot me, do it quickly
If I am to hurt then I am to hurt
I just want to know
Look down dummy, she's right there!

Printed in the United States
By Bookmasters